BEAUTIFUL HUMANS
there's
NOTHING WRONG
with
YOU

Encouragement for the Soul

MARCY BARBARO

 FriesenPress

One Printers Way
Altona, MB R0G 0B0
Canada

www.friesenpress.com

ISBN
978-1-5255-9518-9 (Hardcover)
978-1-5255-9517-2 (Paperback)
978-1-5255-9519-6 (eBook)

1. BIOGRAPHY & AUTOBIOGRAPHY, PERSONAL MEMOIRS

Distributed to the trade by The Ingram Book Company

DEDICATION:

To Dad, who loves a good story, especially the longish ones that catch in your throat during the telling. Your love made this possible.

ACKNOWLEDGEMENTS:

A debt of gratitude to my sister Nancy for encouraging me to tell stories in our bedroom as girls, and for the countless times you have told me that I'm "amazing." I have no idea what I've done to deserve you, but I never want a moment without you within arm's reach.

Thank you to my "big" brother Richard for always making me feel safe, but not for making soup come out of my nose. And to my brother Glen, resting at last, for loving me absolutely.

Thank you, Mom, for Elvis in the mornings, and for being the most creative person I know; a true artist.

I'm grateful to my brother-in-law Dave Hyde for insisting that I get this book done and for never taking no as an answer. You have no idea what your support has meant to me.

My beloved Soul Sista Number One Andrea Stamp: you have been my most constant and longest standing friend. We have to keep each other close at this point, because the stories we could tell would eke out like too much jam between the bread and make a mess everywhere.

Thank you to Jill Woods for your constant good humour, generous heart, and for always prefacing your wisdom with a pause, and addressing me as "Marce" before you begin. This is how I knew the really good stuff was coming.

To Shelley O'Brien for reading every word I wrote, and the comments that improved the copy so much! I will never, ever, tire of your whimsy.

And to the irreplaceable and irrepressible Jennifer McEachen for never understanding why I just didn't finish this thing already. I honestly believe your impatience with my writing process is one of my favourite things about you. Your no-nonsense approach to everything has ushered me along for four decades, made me feel loved, and kept me laughing in the process.

To Jamie Forget and Jeff Halliday, my brothers from other mothers, I love you. I respect you. I learn from you constantly.

To Larissa Mair, I love you for always feeding me, making me laugh, and teaching me so long ago that speaking with a fake accent makes difficult conversations more palatable.

Thank you to Sarah Comeau for sorting through and organizing my early jottings, and for being the best cheerleader ever.

To the two Howies: Uncle Howie for years of endless support, and Howard Akler for teaching me how to pronounce words aloud that I'd only ever read on a page.

And thank you Liza Finlay for your giant brain, and unwavering support of my writing.

To Frankie for more than twenty years of friendship, authentic Italian food, and for sharing your parents with me.

And to the many, many kind souls in the yoga community, a giant thank you for making me realize that the lessons I wove into meditation and *savasana* were of value to everyone.

To Vanessa (Vandenbussche) Fievet for being the most solid human I know, and for always offering to drive.

To Tarra, for constantly believing in the light.

To the Monday Mommies, for all the Mondays, and so much more.

To "Sensei" Kevin, for being one of the best professors I've ever had. "The Iron Never Lies."

To my wise and talented business partner, Alex Morin: you make every conversation filled with ease, and all decisions flow with heart.

To all the book club ladies, thanks for keeping the written word in a place of honour and respect. And to the GGs, Trisha, Karena, and Alex — thanks for listening to my greatest fears and elaborate stories. And, there's truly no one else I'd rather pee in the woods with, as a group.

To my beloved daughter Santana, thank you for catching me when I'm playing small and showing me every day how powerful and beautiful a woman can be. You are a delight.

To my soulful son Luca, your gentle wisdom and superb analytical mind have made me breathless with love and pride more times than I can count. I can't believe you sat and listened to this whole book in one sitting!

To my Lion, Brando, you honour me daily with your unwavering belief in my strength. You are actually the strong one — and I couldn't do any of this without you. It's a pleasure to watch your leadership skills expand. Everyone who meets you remembers you. Oh my angels, you make me want to do more, be more, every day.

And to you, dear reader. Thank you for your leap of faith. Thank you for digging in. Sitting still, and trusting me as your temporary guide. I hope you come away with a nugget.

HOW THIS BOOK CAME TO BE

It happened again. I was setting up for a yoga class in the loft overlooking the water. A student approached, bare feet padding softly. Then she began to speak, eyes locking with mine, and shared what was wrong with her. In this case, it was degenerative disc disease, a common condition, I'd later learn from one of the most prominent physiotherapists and yoga therapists in the country.

But still. This happened almost every time. I'd be cueing up the music, greeting students as they arrived, and invariably be pulled aside for a confessional tête-à-tête.

My doctor says that -
My husband says that -
Or,
I shouldn't do too much of this, because of all these things...
I would do my best to accommodate. I always did.

And yet, my heart broke a little more with each hastily whispered conversation. I sensed their pain was soul deep, instead of just in the superficial layers. This knowledge was a burden dropped so casually onto my sticky mat.

So many people saw themselves in need of repair. So many believed they were broken.

I offered some mobility, breathwork, and a funny story or two; a band-aid that had to be reapplied frequently as it never held in place.

Eventually, my aching heart prompted these questions:
What would happen if I acted as though my students had nothing wrong with them? If I stopped seeing them as broken, would they be able to heal?

I tested a theory I was developing. I became the most gentle and kind teacher I could be. I never pushed. I accepted everything a person could do. I left it at that. It was all good enough.

I didn't know it then, but a door had opened in my thought process, perhaps to my subconscious. I then began to dedicate years to studying mindset, to how our beliefs influence our experiences, to the study of pain, and to achieving forgiveness.

In the process, I plunged the seeds of my personal faith back into the soil under those humble, painted toes. I knew that if I was going to create an environment for healing, I had to do some emotional heavy lifting myself. It was messy. And not quick.

Eventually, I began to share the mindset lessons, as a coach. Today, I help others write books. They are gifts of healing as well, and I'm happy to expand the circle that reaches hearts like limitless hands for holding.

The old me was certain, however, that I was desperately in need of mending, just like some of my yoga clients. This book recounts the personal, high-stakes social experiment of mine, called *Beautiful Humans, There's Nothing Wrong With You.* Let's begin.

LOOKING UP

Oh damn,
I fell down on the journey to self-
worth again today,
paused to notice
my habitually scraped knees,
caked with debris.

From down here
I see all the knees of humanity,
and it's a hard truth,
but they're all banged up, too.

When is enough, enough?
Only self-love stands us up.

And here's a lesson they don't teach
in school:
If hurt people
hurt people,
then healed people
heal people,
too.

CHAPTER 1:
GOGGLES

When I was about fourteen years old, my breasts started to grow.

And grow, and grow, and grow.

In less than a year, I went from being a tall, slim, active kid — doing cartwheels on the lawn, playing baseball, bounding into my backyard pool with confidence — to becoming a self-conscious and eventually heavy fifteen-year-old. I didn't want to run or jump then, because there was so much, well, movement. I slowed down. Like most teenagers, my diet was full of chips and mac'n'cheese and late-night trips to McDonalds. So, I put on weight, and quickly.

In addition to suddenly struggling with confusion around the changes in my body and a lot of new, unexpected attention from men, the biggest issue was how those closest to me began to treat me differently.

My weight gain had become a social issue that everyone felt they had to solve.

"Marcy's gotten fat! Marcy's gotten fat! Marcy is fat — oh what should we do?"

In the 1980s, before the concept of body shaming was realized to be harmful and inappropriate, everyone thought it was their duty to let me know that I had put on weight. School teachers, my uncle, my friends, my mom. It seemed that they could no longer recognize the person I was before the breasts and the weight gain: funny, a good student, creative, and a little sporty. They didn't see that version of me once my outside changed.

And so, I began to see myself differently, too.

That confident, outgoing dreamer, writer, and happy daughter was lost in the fat rolls. And she would not return for many years after a lot of private and not-so-private expressions of pain.

My mom tried her best; she put me on the Scarsdale diet, took me to Weight Watchers, and even dragged me for injections at Dr. Bernstein's clinic. But nothing would work. When anyone would question, "Should you be having that ice cream, Marcy?" I was humiliated. So I would eat more to assuage my pain. "Do you think a bowl of chips while watching *Love Boat* is a good choice?" Never mind that everybody else in the family was eating chips while watching *Love Boat*. Although I'm sure their intentions were good, all I got out of it was that there was something wrong with me.

The way that I dealt with this pain was to act out. My teenage brain interpreted the situation sort of like this: "OK, so hey, if I'm going to be large, then I might as well be larger than life!" I was too young to recognize that my over-eating was stuffing an emotional void.

I'd always had a great sense of humour and could make people laugh. And now I poured my energy into being the clown, who ate sweets and junk, drank alcohol to excess, and made everybody laugh. I laughed, I deflected, I pretended I was OK.

Don't get me wrong, I had a lot of temporary fun during that time and made some great friends, but I also had a new constant companion, who would stick around for almost twenty long years.

That companion was shame.

I had a breast reduction at nineteen and began to exercise. Some of the weight came off as I moved more freely, so the way I was treated changed again. Now, people seemed proud of me. I was more acceptable in my new form, and many expressed admiration over the changes I had made. I lapped up the compliments, although I was tired of others talking about my body.

I'll tell you; I never expected my breasts to be my biggest teacher. (OK, yes, that was supposed to make you smile.) I look back at those days of struggle, amazed at how quickly I had abandoned my own view of myself, internalized what others thought of me, and ultimately tied my self-worth to that myopic vision. I was a ping-pong ball seeking love and attention, impressionable, and easily led.

All those years of people looking at me like I was "worth less" when I was heavy had made me unsure of the truths I had once known about myself. I was then, and still am astonished now, how many unkind remarks I had received when I was heavier.

I recall when living in France as a nanny at eighteen, and being turned away at the doorway of a *United Colors of Benetton* shop.

The sales girl looked me up and down. Gruffly, she muttered, "We have nothing here for you."

The company mandate may have been to accept all colours of skin, but apparently you couldn't get in if you were larger than a size 12.

Sadly, I internalized a lot of those words; swallowing them whole.

The result: I became unsure of the truths I had once known about myself.

And yes, if I had the personal strength at that young age to stand up to the shaming, then perhaps life would have been easier. But I didn't. When I gained weight, I was full of self-loathing. When I lost weight, I felt that I was worth more — worthy of more love, more friendship, more fun, more family, more money.

Thankfully, I'm now able to look back with love at that lost young girl. Her long ride back to self-worth was an angst-ridden movie of questionable characters and bad choices. Yet, she made it. My work as a mindset and writing coach today is all about holding up a mirror to people and saying, *See? You too deserve to be well-loved; you deserve to be loved well.*

I can't say this enough. I will never stop saying it. It was what I so badly needed to hear.

I have never forgotten that young girl's sadness or her fear of being rejected. Poor self esteem meant that her soul was imprisoned by her shape and size. Maybe you've been imprisoned by some old beliefs too?

And you know what would have made the biggest difference to me when I was struggling the most? I'm sure it's the same thing that would make the biggest difference to you now, too.

Answer: If I had realized that there was nothing wrong with me.

I mean, come on. We all want to tweak things a bit, and I'm all for change and personal growth; but at the core, I believe we are all beautiful humans. Period.

That's what this book is about: learning how to form your own view of yourself and stand strong in that conviction of self-worth.

It's full of ideas and practices that help you to shut out others' opinions. To help you move beyond that social currency that was given to you because of how you look, where you're from, whether you were good in school, athletic, or how much money you make — like an imaginary "Hello, My Name Is" badge you can't remove.

The thought process that I outline in this book is a simple concept.

If we think we are flawed and broken, we have to dig ourselves out of a hole just to stand upright.

Regardless of your situation, however, there is nothing wrong with you. Yes, I understand there are medical conditions, and terrible things happen in life that are real, and there are sometimes painful obstacles to work through. But that is all on the outside. Like my large breasts, it might be a part of you, but it's not the genuine you at the core.

The real you at the core is powerful, 100 percent unique, and full of remarkable potential. And, oh yes, also divine. You know you are more than the sum of your physical parts. You are sparks and spirit with a voice all your own. It's easy to forget, but it's true.

And yes, I know the messages to the contrary are many. Entire industries are built on making you feel like you are less, right? The noise is constant. It can be hard to tune-in to your true self and listen, when you've been told something by so many, for so long. But I'm here to tell you that something can be done. And something needs to be done! If you stick with me and learn how to listen to your own perfect soul, you'll begin receiving the opposite of those messages. That's the station you need to tune-in to. All the time.

If I can develop the capacity to get out from under the shame that took root in me, and do the work to live freely and joyfully as I do now — then you can do it, too.

Let's dig in. Let's start right now, Beautiful Humans.

PUTTING IN THE WORK: THE FAVOURITE PHOTOGRAPH MEDITATION

So, I don't care who you are, or where you were born, but there were moments as a child in which you knew 100 per cent who you were. Sure, you didn't have the self-reflection or the language to articulate that exactly, but instinctively you knew what made you happy: playing in the dirt organizing pebbles, drawing, jumping boundlessly, sitting quietly and observing.

We had a radar — I know you remember that radar — that moved us towards certain things and away from others.

We had an inherent understanding about which situations, people, and practices made us feel good, whole, powerful, unique, and valued and which ones didn't. Let's find that version of yourself again. Do this practice below, and I'm sure you'll find access.

I have often used this practice in my yoga classes, just as my students are settling into *savasana* — the lying down and relaxing part at the end of the yoga class. You don't have to have done yoga, or even like yoga, for this to work for you.

But just as a bit of background for the uniniti-ated, savasana is where the magic happens. After all of the conscious breathing in and out and opening, rotating, and lengthening we do with our bodies in a typical yoga class, then we lie down and rest and the mind is often remarkably clear. This practice of savasana is highly addictive; number one, because it just feels so darn good to stop and lie down as an adult, but also because over time, during this rest, we often have a revelation about some particular area of our lives that is working or not working, and these moments of clarity become catalysts for change.

And so, back to the photograph. Now I understand that not everyone is a visual person, so if you can't visualize an image of yourself per se, then I want you to use your other senses to remember. Grab hold of that image of your favourite picture of yourself, or that memory, and try to remember how you were feeling during that time.

How old were you?

Where were you?

What were you wearing?

What were you doing?

Were you indoors or outside?

Were you moving or still?

Take some breaths and tap into it. If you are experiencing some negative talk right now, such as, "How am I supposed to remember?" or "My parents worked so much, we never went anywhere, so I don't have any good memories," I need you to set all of that aside.

In order for this process of moving towards joy to happen within your being, you're going to have to try something different.

So, close your eyes, breathe, and get still. Let it happen. See yourself clearly, as you were then.

THE MIRROR

Way back in the '70s,
They took my favourite picture of me:

Yellow T-shirt with The Fonz,
Chin lifted to keep that big cowboy
hat on
Fearlessly leaning
against Uncle David's horse
All smiles and flies,
and big blue eyes
free in the meadow
trusting the unknown,
safety and rapture
so at home.

And so, how did it go for you?

Did you find that kid?

Did you like that person? (If you didn't, were those someone else's words reverberating through your mind? Watch for this!)

What did you like about that being?

What qualities come to mind to describe yourself as you were then?

And how did others respond to you? How would people describe you back then?

This is actually a great time to put down this book and to journal. If you've never journaled before, don't overthink it. You don't need to go out and buy a pretty hardcover book and stow it between your mattresses each night. Any old drugstore notebook will do, because it's the insides of that book that count (kind of like who you truly are).

Don't make the journal too precious. I mean, it's precious because the words inside are coming from you, but it's not so precious because that implies that it must be preserved forever. And guess what? You're evolving here, and in a few years you might go back and read it and think, *Yikes, who is this person?* and want to set the journal on fire. And guess what? You can do that, too, if that feels right.

> As an aside here: because I've been a writer my whole life, people have constantly gifted me the most gorgeous notebooks. Like, for the past forty years. I love each and every one of them, but to be truthful, I was terrified to write in the nice ones. I didn't want to mess up the pages with my imperfect, rambling words, and I certainly didn't think that I could fill the thing! I hesitated to commit my poetry and journaling to such nice pages, and those pretty, high-quality notebooks remained empty for years. Over time, thank goodness, I got over that way of thinking. I'm sharing my experience in case you're hesitating to put pen to paper.

Now if you don't want to journal, that's OK too. But I hope that you took the time to immerse yourself in that past version of yourself. Let your imagination go, and the gates to your deeply hidden self swing open.

I remember when my daughter was born. I was in the hospital staring into her face and a nurse said to me, *See her eyes? Those will never change.* I loved that.

And I'll tell you something else that never changes: your spirit. That spark. That you before you even understood who you were. Before you became labelled and self-conscious and got lost in overthinking and the shoulds.

Yup. That's you, Beautiful Human.

And this is the first piece of the puzzle to putting yourself all back together into one amazing whole.

I had a remarkable, gorgeous woman actually start crying one evening in a private yoga session with me. She had made a lot of recent changes to her life, and she was just so darn tired and overwhelmed by all of the new, new, new.

I just hung out with her as she cried, and we did some gentle movement and restorative poses, her eyes raining big drops down her face all the while, pausing to blow her nose when needed. She left feeling better and emailed me later that night to thank me for allowing her to express her feelings so safely.

My reply to her was, "You're going to be OK. Enjoy the falling apart because when you put yourself back together it's going to be with the strongest 'Don't f*** with me' glue, ever."

We laughed. I know a lot of women who love to swear. I guess after years of being told that we should be nice, it feels great to use words that are offensive or unexpected, at times.

Anyway, to you, dear reader, I say don't be afraid to fall apart a bit. Say what you want to say, push the edges of who you think you are supposed to be, and get back to who you know you are.

If you're reading this book, then something in your life isn't working.

You crave change. And, you have to break yourself up a bit in order to reassemble things in a new way. Am I right? The good news is you're not the only one doing this. We all have to do it if we want to live differently. If we want to *be* different.

Just a note about change:

It isn't that easy. That's why so few do it. We'd often rather suffer with what's familiar rather than wade through the discomfort of change. Our subconscious challenges us. We are fearful and feel alone, wishing we'd never stepped out of our box, wanting to scurry back in at the first sign of resistance.

And it's common for those closest to us — our family members, co-workers, and best friends to mount the most resistance to us changing. Generally, it's because they love us as we are and are suspicious of who we'll become.

Indeed, in her spectacular book, *Finding Your Own North Star*,[1] Martha Beck details how to find our inner compass and follow it. A former Ph.D. academic, Beck shifted her focus from valuing the intellect first and foremost, to pursuing a life of inner gifts when she discovered she was carrying a son who would be born with Down's Syndrome. Beck is a beacon of strength and wisdom. I just love her.

---

1   Martha Beck, *Finding Your Own North Star: Claiming the Life You Were Meant to Live* (New York: Three Rivers Press, 2001).

One of the exercises in her book instructs us how to make a specific and powerful vision board on a large roll of newsprint paper. Then, Beck mentions that the reader may need to take the vision board down and roll it up before family members see it, lest they be discouraging in some way. I was surprised when I read this, but I get it.

In fact, my girl, the hilarious and wise, Jen Sincero, explains it best in her book, *You Are a Badass at Making Money: Master the Mindset of Wealth,* as to why we may need to protect ourselves and our dreams sometimes:[2]

> Make an effort to surround yourself with people who cheer you on and offer support, not who hand you a 'Good luck with that' bag of turds, or the ole favourite, 'I'm telling you these (negative) things because I'm worried about you, I'm just trying to help.' That's basically them saying, 'I'm small and scared and I'm rubbing it all over you, but you can't object because it means I care.' Worriers, doubters, freakers, sad sacks, small thinkers, complainers, naysayers, whiners, chunters, grumpers, scaredy cats — these are not the people you want to share your dreams with.

You can still love these people and have them in your life, Sincero says, but like Beck, believes it may be good practice to keep some of your personal growth activities to yourself.

You may be experiencing some of this resistance from those close to you right now, and probably resent the heck out of

---

2   Jen Sincero, *You Are a Badass at Making Money: Master the Mindset of Wealth* (New York: Penguin Books, 2017) p. 190.

them for it. I understand. And yet, that's some pretty poo-poo energy to carry around inside of you when you are trying to soar with the eagles. Fear not, after the next chapter we will delve into another healing process essential to loving your fine self and everybody else: the practice of forgiveness. In the meantime, your job is to flex a little faith. Actually who'm I kidding? A whole lotta faith.

In his book, *The War on Art: Break Through the Blocks and Win Your Inner Creative Battles*, author Steven Pressfield lists resistance, fear, and isolation as our frequent companions on the journey to personal growth, and yet, as we pursue our soul's purpose, we develop another source of strength in the process.

He writes:

> Here's the trick: We're never alone. As soon as we step outside the campfire glow, our Muse lights on our shoulder like a butterfly. The act of courage calls forth infallibly that deeper part of ourselves that supports and sustains us.[3]

Call it a muse, faith, trust, belief. Choose your word for it but that deeper part of ourselves is more than bones and flesh. We know that we're supported by something unseen. Powerful.

God, Goddess, Infinite Intelligence, the Universe, and Spirit of Your Ancestors, may all sound like different entities, but they amount to faith in the unknown. This faith will also be a part of your journey here. I encourage you to unearth the path to that garden and let it grow.

---

3   Steven Pressfield, *The War on Art: Break Through the Blocks and Win Your Inner Creative Battles* (New York : Black Irish Entertainment, 2002), p. 44.

GETTING A GRIP

There are times
when I must grab my own ass with
two hands
and drag myself into action

There are times
when I have let fear weigh me down
like an old boyfriend's forgotten sweater
and I curl up on the couch of life
certain —
that I will never be brilliant again
or light again, or sexy or powerful or
capable again

But then, gripping my ass as such
I feel ridiculous,
and laugh that laugh
that frees me
moves me forward
and reminds me
that I already hold everything
I need to know.

CHAPTER 2:
HOW TO BE INSTANTLY RICH

So the seeds of this book were planted over a lifetime. Those of you who create know. I've come to call this process "percolating," probably because I love brewed hot bevvies so much. When you put everything in, add some heat and some time, then good stuff comes out, a perfect alchemy to support quiet contemplation, meaningful conversation; watching the birds. Hope in a cup.

I never thought anything I was doing was particularly remarkable over the past twenty plus years — raising my kids, working out at the gym, being a yoga teacher, eating healthy food, writing some poetry — but at the time when I'd begun posting a lot on Instagram and Facebook, I would receive messages frequently, from both friends and people I'd never met.

"You are always so positive; how do you do it?"
"You inspire me to do better, to be better."
"How do you keep from giving up?"
"I need to spend time with you, so you can teach me this stuff."

I was like, *Wow. You guyssss.* I actually still feel the same way when I receive that kind of message, so humbled by it and a tiny bit confused, because I have struggled. I have given up. I mean, I'm fifty-four, and I'm finally writing this book.

All of these questions got me thinking. Maybe something I'm doing is a bit unique. Maybe my outlook is worth looking into. I don't consider myself someone who inspires people, so I began to dig.

I wondered, *Why do I always wake up in a good mood? Why do I like most people I meet, even when I can see that they are being a jerk, or fearful and insecure, or judgmental?* Perhaps part of it is the temperament with which I was born.

People are a lot like puppies in that respect. Some dogs are goofy and friendly, while others are wary and meek right from the get-go. One friend described me as a retriever who bounds up to others, sniffing crotches, always eager to make friends and play.

I realize that this is the whole nurture versus nature argument here and I'm not going to explore that too deeply. I just think we're all born with a way of being. Of course we can change that if we want. That's why books like this are written. In the meantime, we're busy living with what we've got. And sometimes our natural bark and wag is sweeter and tamer than most, and sometimes it's not.

Case in point: I have a book that was given to me as a goodbye gift from my favourite Grade 3 teacher in Geraldton, Ontario, when I was moving to Barrie (*Southern* Ontario, yo! They have more than two months of warm weather a year!) and the inscription in the book was addressed to me as "Little Miss Sunshine." Call it coincidence, but I've been called that so many times in my life! I've also been told I was a "bright light." (I was also told *very* often that I talk too much, too. Ouch! But more on that later.) In any case, this is not a persona that I put on while I secretly nurse my anger over whisky, nightly. I'm generally always in a good mood, and I thrive on connecting with people.

Point being, I thought everyone was this way. I truly had a hard time articulating my philosophy or temperament, until the day I came across a passage quoting Lynne Twist in Brene Brown's book, *The Gifts of Imperfection: Let Go of Who You Think You're Supposed to Be and Embrace Who You Are.*[4]

My mind was blown. Brown was trying to make a point about the difference between living from a place of scarcity or a place of abundance, which Twist calls "sufficiency" in her book.

I'm paraphrasing here, but basically Twist points out that for many of us, when we wake up in the morning, our first thoughts are that we didn't get enough sleep, that we don't have enough time, that we probably won't get enough exercise that day, or enough time in nature, or laugh enough, or make enough money to get ahead, or, or, or — you get the gist of it.

On days when I felt world-weary, sure, those were the first thoughts that popped into my head when my eyes opened. I'd spend each day just trying to be a good mom and maybe earn a bit of money. I did indeed suffer from this common thought process.

On many other days of my life, however, I woke up freaking excited to be alive, and for no particular reason. I just felt that everything was really, really good in my world. Twist's mind-blowing wisdom consolidated a welcome and simple understanding of the thinking and temperament that I'd had forever. And this understanding has resulted in cultivating an

---

4   Brené C. Brown, *The Gifts of Imperfection: Let Go of Who You Think You're Supposed to Be and Embrace Who You Are* (Center City, Minnesota: Hazeldon Publishing, 2010), pp. 82–84.

even stronger feeling of utter freedom over my time. I was onto something, but I needed to know more.

I sought out Lynne Twist's book, *The Soul of Money: Transforming Your Relationship with Money and Life*,[5] and the wisdom within those pages extended beyond teaching about money. The author so cleanly articulated a knowing that I had within. Many of you have this too, I'm certain. Twist says, if we look at everything we have from a place of lack; a place of not enough, then despite what we may accumulate financially or otherwise, there will actually never be enough. Additionally, we will actually never *be* enough either.

Here's the crux of it: in her many visits to both impoverished countries across the globe, and also with some of the world's most wealthy people while fundraising for *The Hunger Project*, Twist learned that being "rich" or "poor" had actually very little to do with how much money one possesses.

If you *feel* like you have everything you need, then you feel *rich* (a sense of sufficiency). If you feel *fearful* about how much you have or don't have all the time, then you will feel *poor* (a sense of lack).

The author stayed in remote communities where residents worked together to create a common goal and had little actual money, yet felt wealthy — in relationships, in their homes, in their abilities to thrive. She also spent time with those whole life purpose was to protect their family inheritance and fortune. Often those people felt isolated, anxious, and struggled with substance misuse due to a sense of scarcity and fear every day.

---

5   Lynne Twist, *The Soul of Money: Transforming Your Relationship with Money and Life* (New York: W. W. Norton and Company, 2017).

Bottom line: how much money you have in the bank does not determine what's enough. Only your mindset does.

When you live from a place of sufficiency, you are always rich. And the good news is we have the ability to change our mindset from not having enough, not being enough, and always seeking more, to knowing that we are sufficient in every moment.

All you have to do is pay attention to where your thoughts go around certain things. Practise feeling deep joy and gratitude for everything that you get to do.

You don't *have to* eat vegetables. You *get to* eat them and fuel your body with rich nutrients.

You don't have to go to the gym and sweat. When you work out with your friends, walk into the gym knowing you're already enough, just as you are. Sweat for fun. Because you can.

When you feel this way, life is full of joy, and you set yourself free.

OK, you say, enough with the sunshine and rainbows. You identify as one of the mean, wary dogs, because life hasn't always been easy for you. We all have something to overcome; that challenges us to grow. Remember that I grew enormous breasts unexpectedly and was tsk tsk'd for contracting the "disease" of obesity. Man, I was *pissed*. I faltered, and spent a long time wallowing in victimhood.

So, we start where we are. Let's just see if we can shift the stone from your heart or at least unfurl your snarled eyebrow.

Start with an honest personal inventory, and then begin a regular practice of gratitude.

I'm one of those people who never remembers jokes, but this one has always stuck with me:

"How many psychologists does it take to change a lightbulb?

Answer: Only one, but the lightbulb has to want to change."

Do you want to change? Or do you want to stay stuck and only half living your life, grumbling along and blaming others for the lack? The choice is yours, but I'm here to tell you that there's nothing wrong with you to begin with. When you set your mind on sufficiency — being enough and having enough, then that's exactly what happens. It's a daily practice, to be truthful. If you do it, things will shift, I promise. You've got to get the guitar out of the case, and practise your chords daily, pressing your tender fingertips into the strings against the frets. You've got to develop those tough little calluses if you want to make music.

The practice of gratitude is the practice of getting extraordinarily good at noticing all the little things that are happening right in this moment, this moment, this moment.

Right now as you read this, can you see out of both eyes? Let's say you can't. Perhaps you have the technology to listen to an audiobook or use a reader? So, we've established that you are possibly visually impaired, but do you have two legs that work? Are you funny? Do you have someone to love? Or do you have an extraordinary gift of caring for houseplants? Did someone call you up out of the blue today? Is your bed comfortable? Do you have access to water, heat, good food, and sometimes delicious butter tarts?

The practice of gratitude is the most transformative habit you will ever develop. It's like seeing the world in a new way, all the time. We want to train our minds to believe that we are living all the time from a place of sufficiency — a place of enough.

I feel confident enough to share my layman's scientific understanding of emotional frequency, so here it goes:. Every emotion has an actual frequency, or corresponding vibration in the body. Not surprisingly, emotions such as anger, hatred, shame and fear have some of the lowest vibrations and, obviously, love, gratitude, compassion and joy have some of the highest ones.

When we vibrate at a higher frequency, we feel better and some say we heal more easily. Before you think this is all a little too woo-woo for you, I'm going to give you two examples that remind you that you already know what I'm talking about when I mention vibration.

We've all walked into a room where there is tension, where someone was "having words" just before we arrived. The anger is hanging in the air, and if you're like me, you want to turn around and walk right back out when this happens.

Here's another scenario: you're at a table in a pub with your friends, and the server is nowhere to be found, so you go up to the bar to grab a round for everyone. Your friends are, of course, delighted with your generosity and initiative, and in this relaxed setting, proceed to tell jokes and funny stories while waiting. When you return, drinks in hand, you see smiles and looks of laughter on people's faces. But it's mostly the crackle in the air that indicates to you a sense of fun.

"What did I miss?" you inquire, smirking already.

It's emotional frequency. And that's a straight-up palatable thing.

There are gratitude journals and gratitude practices everywhere online and so much stuff written about this, so there's no need for me to get into a lot of how-to detail here. Every day, several times a day, however, pay attention to the dialogue in your mind. Do you run a loop, reciting all of the rotten things that are happening in the world? Is that the piece of gristle that you chew on day in and day out? OK, so stop.

Start replacing those thoughts consciously with something good. The sun is shining. Someone held the door for you. You can hear the laughter of the neighbour's kids as they play outside. Your team won last night. All of your socks found a match.

Your job is to become the super-noticer of all things amazing.

Write them down if you want. Snap a quick pic with your phone and post these moments on your socials with the hashtag #beautifulhumans if that helps you to remember, but pour all the goodness in, all the time, and then see what happens. You are going to be so incredibly surprised how this simple activity changes your emotional signature and attracts all kinds of fun, exciting moments to your life.

I know I'm throwing a lot at you here, but all of this stuff is doable and actually works! And it's free. When I think of you, dear reader, I already think you're amazing. You have something unique to offer this world and you're on the planet to do that thing so well and in a way that only you can do. The problem is that most of us suffer from a lack of belief in what we can do, who we can be, and what we can have. So begin to inventory all day, every day, the goodness around you. It's a helluva confidence builder.

This new habit will be the biggest driver to sufficiency that you've ever experienced.

Decide to say bye-bye to that sad, disappointing sense of lack for good and see *the plenty* around you. That will result in feeling a richness in your moments. Your shoulders will drop, your chest will lift, and you will be enough — for yourself, and subsequently for everyone else too.

In *Ayurveda*, the ancient sister science to yoga, one belief is that everything is food. The music we listen to, the books we read, what we watch, the conversations we have, the quality of the air we breathe — everything gets into our cells, nourishing or depleting them.

I ask you, what are you feeding yourself? Would you call what you are putting in "nourishment"? If you haven't done so in the past, start now.

Honour your beautiful self ... would you just?

PUTTING IN THE WORK:
FORGIVENESS MEDITATION

One of the stories we often tell ourselves is that it's not so easy to change. The reason I share some of my pain in this book isn't to elicit your sympathy. It's to remind you that we all have experiences that trip us up in life.

We're born sweet, and full of love, and then someone tells us that we run too slowly, or our singing voice is horrible, our ears stick out, we have a medical condition, an unhealthy parent, and one or more of these things interrupt us mid-cartwheel. The pain sets in, and we may flounder for years, bewildered and seeking safety.

Sadly, the default setting appears to be that we feel that we are not enough.

Even if we do find loving relationships in our adult life and develop the skills to overcome what we were previously criticized for, the hurt is still there and buried deep. I can't tell you how many clients I've had, who were "not good in school," and they carried this with them for years.

Someone somewhere told them they were "dumb," and as adults they held their breath, not living to the fullest expression of themselves as they waited for the next poor report card to come from a work supervisor, from their lover, or on the monthly bank statement. Those early comments affected how they saw themselves, eroded their confidence, and ultimately held them back from expanding in all of the ways they could.

Before we can move forward, we need to forgive the past. This is the next exercise in this book, and it's so integral to lifting your heart and easing your pain. Yes, we have to forgive others, but we must also forgive ourselves for those times of doubt and weakness, or for simply not showing-up for ourselves the way that we are prepared to today.

> The ancient Hawaiian prayer called Ho'oponopono is a beautiful practice of healing and reconciliation that operates on the assumption that we are all connected. So, even when we are the ones who have been wronged, this meditation begins with an apology, because love and forgiveness for others and love and forgiveness for ourselves are ultimately the same thing.

I need you to trust me on this. This works so well.

Get out your journal again and write down all of the terrible things that were said to you and how you were hurt throughout your lifetime. I know it seems counterproductive to go backwards and unearth all that you have buried so deeply. Yet, we know for certain that holding those memories in your body are not helping you. It's now common knowledge that releasing emotional pain is essential to your well-being. If these last couple of phrases fascinate you, then I highly recommend you read Dr. Gabor Maté's groundbreaking book, *When The Body Say No; The Cost of Hidden Stress.*

What's on your list? What do you need to forgive yourself for?

Write lovingly, with empathy, as though holding something precious in your hands. You may feel exhausted and need a nap, to go for a walk in nature, or hydrate, during this process.

If this is the case, leave it for now, and come back when your energy is topped-up.

The next step begins when you've completed your list.

One by one, read each item, and slowly recite *Ho'oponopono*:

I am sorry.

Forgive me.

Thank you.

I love you.

Go to the next item and repeat the forgiveness phrases slowly and mindfully.

Keep going down the list. Hold space for, and release each one.

Repeat the process with the sticky memories, too, until eventually you feel a lightness in your chest around them all. This healing is not instantaneous, and yet, we are moving in the right direction. For example, if you always quarrel with one of your siblings, the next time she or he calls, you might notice less tension between you, or you might not get as stirred-up by previously triggering words. This is progress. Perhaps do the forgiveness practice again.

Also, I've seen slight variations in the words used in this practice, and the four phrases are in a different order sometimes, too. I don't think that's especially important. The main thing is to own your feelings and personal narrative. Then, experience how absolutely powerful it is to send love and forgiveness to someone who has hurt you, and also back to yourself.

Good for you.

You have done more soul work. You are moving closer to a life of vitality and joy.

EXTREME ATHLETE OF THE HEART

I often describe each of my friends as
my best friend,
and my favourite child is always
the one
who my eyes are on at that moment.

A good time is always the best time,
and every first bite of cake is
more delicious
than the last first one.

I will engage in conspiratorial conversation with a pal of thirty years
with the intensity of a first meeting,
and pull on a lover's lips
as if we won't ever kiss again.

I live on the pinnacles —
suck in all the thin air at the
highest heights
and live dizzy all the time.

The cautious types would say this can't
be sustained,
shouldn't be really,
but I've been riding this high,
sometimes closing my eyes,

sticky with fear inside.

You know, I can't downhill ski
and I sure as hell can't surf,
but I am a different kind
of gold-medallist,
a peak, extreme athlete of the heart.

CHAPTER 3:
YOU GET WHAT YOU SEE

On this journey to wholeness, we all have helpers. Those people are our "ride or die" besties, who believe in us at our worst, even when we don't believe in ourselves. They love us when we are not so pretty — when ugly words fall out of our mouths, when we are confused and weak, when we make bad decisions from a place of fear, and when we're just plain not nice.

It happens. We're human.

What I'm describing here is unconditional love.

That's the opposite of love with conditions: *I love you only when you are a shiny bright diamond and crushing it in all areas of your life...*

Not that kind of love. The other. Do you know what I mean? Do you have a family member, spouse, mentor, or childhood friend who is that for you? Well, for me, that person is my dad. Bear with me here while I introduce him to you, and you'll get some good stuff at the end of the story, too.

When I was a child, my dad had a habit in the morning of flinging open the glass sliding door to the backyard and shouting, *Hello World!* into the fresh air. When I was younger, it was delightful; as a teenager, it was dreadfully embarrassing. Even as I screwed up my face in disapproval, my dad never stopped doing this.

He'd also get up in the middle of the night completely naked and go to the kitchen for a couple of Oreos. If you accidentally got up at the same time to use the washroom or get a drink of water, you'd get a flash of his white butt as he stood there, cookies cupped in his hand, looking out the kitchen window, and delighting in his midnight treat. He might catch your eye mischievously as though to say, *Don't tell anyone I'm just a big kid, too,* and you'd head back to bed embarrassed, but also somehow comforted by this.

What I haven't mentioned here is that my father was a police officer for twenty-seven years. Yup. And despite what he undoubtedly saw and experienced in that line of work, he remains to this day the most jolly, light-hearted person you'll ever meet.

He didn't bring his work home with him. He was quiet sometimes and always a deep thinker and soft talker, but was never brooding or sad. You expected him to be different — grumpy or sarcastic and disheartened like some of his fellow officers were during visits to the house. How he could remain so level became a mystery to me as I grew a little older.

Mustering my courage to pry into adult affairs, one day I asked him straight out:

"Dad, is your job hard?"

He paused, considering, then answered with a sigh:

"Well, dear, all I can tell you is that we drive right on by the houses where all of the happy people live."

Now in his late seventies, my father has a strong faith that he draws upon. But when I was younger, I never saw him read the Bible. He always had this lightness about him, though. He was, and is, my most influential teacher. By his constant buoyant mood, he demonstrates that despite challenging experiences **we can always decide how we're going to show up in the world**. He's a huge believer in laughing at yourself, your frailties and blunders, and that if you want good, then you need to find the good.

You get what you see.

He also taught me that a little conversation with a shop owner can go a long way.

In the early 1980s, my father used to stop-in at a little convenience store in the mornings to grab a cup of coffee as the sun was coming up. It was one of the only places open that early, and he still had a few hours in the squad car to go.

To hear the story now, when my dad was paying for his cup of coffee, he noticed that the store owner had the cash from the till all laid out on the counter. He was adding up the revenue from the night before and preparing his bank deposit. My father couldn't help but comment to the store owner how risky he thought this was, and how likely it was that he'd get robbed. Disgruntled, the shop owner told my father that he was a one-man show. He put in a lot of hours at the store, and dawn was the safest time to do the bookkeeping.

To say these two men didn't hit it off was an understatement. My father took his coffee and left, annoyed at the man's stupidity. Returning to his work, the convenience store owner was noticeably irritated by the nosy cop.

My father must have been tired that morning, because he generally finds the good in every situation. More in line with his character, the next day while on the same shift, he returned to the store. He was a bit lighter in mood and armed with a solution.

There was a ripple of tension as my father entered in full police uniform. In fact, the shop owner sighed in exasperation as he anticipated another dressing down from the constable while he carried out his bookkeeping. Instead, my father poured himself a cup of coffee, fixed it as he liked it, most likely a little giddy at the anticipated conversation, and then leaned back on the sturdiest shop shelf he could find, taking a sip. The shopkeeper looked up, surprised at this police officer who showed no sign of leaving.

"I'm Murray," my dad said then, thrusting his hand forward. "And if you need to count your money with the shop open every day at this hour, then I guess I'll have my morning coffee here."

And so began a rich and remarkable friendship that spanned many decades.

Even on his days off, my father consistently arose early and drove to the shop to have a cup of coffee with his now dear friend, Alex. Oh, the conversations and laughs they would have in that hour. Alex was from Newfoundland and Labrador, possessed a great wit, and was a compelling storyteller. Their friendship grew to such an extent that they both looked forward to their daily visits, discussing parenting, marriage, and the sometimes-puzzling intricacies of life.

They rarely saw each other outside of that setting. The convenience store counter between them interacted as both church confessional and bar in a neighbourhood pub, depending on where the conversation took them. A safe place where souls were poured out openly and conversations ran long and deep.

When Alex eventually died of cancer, attending his funeral with my dad was one of the proudest moments of my life. It was so clear to me how my dad's ability to see the good in people created this expansive and beautiful friendship that ended up being such a profoundly powerful and now bittersweet gift.

This is just one example of how my father taught me about moments. Moments are everything. They are the beads of experience that we string on our own necklaces of life, but *only* if we're wise enough to catch the glimmer of them in any light.

We think a simple exchange means nothing, and yet it can mean everything. Our perspective on the thing, how our heart sits in our chests, our intentions heading in, our ability to problem-solve when all we want to do is run, and to always, always, always, see the best in people — this is where the richness of life comes from. When we see people as whole and as worthy of our time and attention, then that's who they will be.

Yes, I understand that there are times when others let us down. Each person is on his or her own path, and the route from start to finish is never a straight line. Wires get crossed. And no one likes to touch a hot stove.

Most times, however, when we see ability and abundance, we create it.

We get what we see.

We create how we live.

Instead of my father avoiding that shop and waiting for the "foolish" shop owner to be robbed, he saw a man doing the best he could with the resources he had and met him there.

This is what we can do daily if we choose to. I dare say it's what we need to do if we want a rewarding life, full of joy.

It's so easy to see the difference between others and ourselves. For many of us, this is a reflex. And so, I challenge you.

The next time you feel like pulling away from someone who feels so different from you, or someone whom you don't understand, instead move towards that person.

One of the most health-giving practices you can do is to see the similarities between others and yourself. Then draw the line to connect the two.

Find something in that person that looks like you.
Lean in.
See the like.
Feel the like.
How does that show up in your body, in your heart?
It feels light, doesn't it?
Enjoy this and make it a daily practice of yours. Now, you are on the path to happiness, to love.
You get what you see.

PUTTING IN THE WORK: LEANING IN AND MAKING THE MOMENTS COUNT

May you be safe. May you be happy. May you be well. May you live with ease.

Think of someone in your life who "rubs you the wrong way." Most often, we are repelled by people or situations that represent something that we do not like within ourselves.

Here's the hard part: the next time you are with that person, figure out what bugs you the most. Now, be honest, does that quality exist in you too? Or is that a quality that you have recently worked hard to overcome? Do you worry deep down that by letting this person in you will somehow regress to that state?

Before you do anything, let's first of all practice metta meditation. This is also known as the Loving-Kindness Meditation, and it's been around *forever*. So, if you want to learn more about it, you can easily look it up. But jump on in, because here's how you do it:

We always begin the metta meditation by directing it towards ourselves. It's good to practise self-love, and we get weary sometimes, so this is a nice way to top up the tank.

<u>Close your eyes and repeat these four phrases to yourself, while sitting or lying still and quiet:</u>

May I be safe.

May I be happy.

May I be well.

May I live with ease.

Don't rush this.

Take your time, and let these beautiful, healing words wash over you, sink into you. Repeat this again, taking your time and relaxing into them. Let these words be a salve for your banged up heart.

Next, call to mind someone you love profoundly, or who has had a positive influence on you in some way. Think of that person's name, get a picture of his or her face in your mind, and repeat the Loving-Kindness Meditation again.

May you be safe.

May you be happy.

May you be well.

May you live with ease.

Repeat once more.

Next, we direct the metta meditation to someone in our lives who we may not know very well but see often. This could be the cashier at the grocery store, a neighbour you see in passing, a co-worker you say hello to but have never actually sat down and had lunch with. Eyes closed, breathing evenly, repeat the above words twice.

Now, here's the hard one. I need you to think of someone that you are in conflict with, or you simply avoid for some reason, that rubs you the wrong way. Draw the image of that person's face into your mind or say their name softly on your lips. Keep your breath steady and begin:

May you be safe.

May you be happy.

May you be well.

May you live with ease.

Now, do it again.

My experience has always been that by the time I get through the meditation the second time, I no longer can hold the image of that person's face or their name in my head. I have actually let go! It amazes me every time.

At this point, with a clearer conscience and a lighter heart, we can expand our reach with our Loving-Kindness thoughts and intentions. Call to mind an entire country, a region of the world, an organization that you support, a group, a gathering, a segment of the population that you wish to send love and healing to. Repeat the mantras again twice, while holding this group you've chosen in your heart. In this way, messages are received, and some healing is done.

Call it prayer, call it mantra, call it intention, call it love — call it whatever you want, but it's quantum physics that states that we were all one molecule that got broken apart and so as such, we all are pieces of the other.

Mother Teresa's famous quote about peace echoes this sentiment perfectly: "If we have no peace, it is because we have forgotten that we belong to each other."

I always wrap up my metta practice by returning the focus on myself again. It's a nice, reassuring way to close the energy loop and love yourself just a little bit more, so why not?

May I be safe.

May I be happy.

May I be well.

May I live with ease.

This practice is older than I am, and bigger than us all. Keep an open mind. Almost everyone I've ever done this with has been moved to tears by the end.

Our thoughts and intentions create so much of our reality and attract or repel the energy that establishes our quality of life.

So, let's declutter this cupboard! Open up your heart. Move forward and release existing patterns of behaviour and limiting beliefs. Make room on the shelf for the new.

YOU

In that light, in this moment,
I see —
your very spirit pushing the edges of
your skin suit,
threatening escape —
Your laughter is a bark that
causes delight,
and simultaneously makes one wish
they had ear plugs in.
You've got so much good
juice flowing,
that it spills out of your gleaming eyes,
your sparkling mouth,
lubricating ease between all.
That's right, Baby,
be big,
as big as you wanna be, need to be.
I celebrate you,
because not one bit of you
makes me less
Me.

CHAPTER 4:
THAT WONDROUS SUITCASE
THAT CARRIES YOUR SOUL

Yes, I'm talking about your body.

Your meat-suit.

Your external package. Or, as I like to say, that wondrous suitcase that carries your soul.

There was a time when I was so disconnected from my body that I was basically moving through the world as a metaphoric head on a stick. In a society that glamourizes intellect, this is pretty easy to do, and in many ways encouraged. How many times have you heard someone described as maybe a bit less than a good person, but their moral shortfalls are swept under the rug with the exclamation, "Yeah, but she or he's so smart, though"?

Why do we *love* smart people so much? Well, they can teach us things. And at the most basic level we sense that our survival skills are enhanced, perhaps leading to a longer and more fruitful life. Additionally, as our skills and intellect grow, oftentimes so does our bank account.

To most, smarts = value = security.

And so, we live in our heads. We oft ignore the cells from the neck down unless they become unwell, only paying attention when the discomfort becomes bad enough to distract us from our intellectual quest.

But I want to talk about your body. Let's tap into that remarkable continuous system that keeps your revered brain alive.

How do you feel about your body at this exact moment? Do you feel strong, attractive, sexy, energetic; just plain old happy with what you've got?

Or did you just freak out a little when I asked that question?

Before you close this book abruptly and head to the cupboard to dive into a box of cookies, let's dwell here together for a bit. Loving our bodies is tough. If I were to send a survey out into the world at this moment, I bet the numbers would come back pretty low on those who would say, "Yes! I love myself from the hairs on my head (or lack of) to the cracked heels of my feet!"

I'm not here to tell you to exercise more. If you've had the same experience as I have, I'm certain that you have been told to "exercise and eat right" pretty much every damn day of your adult life.

And sadly you may secretly look at your body as I once did — as a constant reminder of all of the ways that you have let yourself down.

But what if a shift was created that made you *want* to move your body more? That made you want to choose good, nourishing, healthy food? That naturally over time, took this spectacular set of remarkable automatic systems that live within you, and brought them to optimal function? That would be pretty darn cool, wouldn't it?

So, let's begin with one question:

How do you want to feel?

This concept was first introduced to me by the mega-famous and super-wise owl glasses lady, Danielle LaPorte, in her book, *The Firestarter Sessions: A Soulful & Practical Guide to Creating Success on Your Own Terms.*[6]

I mean, if you want to see a book that is marked up, under-lined, highlighted, and filled with Post-it notes, you should see my copy of that book. It is beloved by me. *Beloved.* I've cracked open so many of my heart's desires while working through that book.

PUTTING IN THE WORK: (YES, ALREADY!) JOURNALLING: HOW DO YOU WANT TO FEEL?

Get your journal out, or just simply sit there right now with your eyes closed for a minute. Remove any other distractions.

In an ideal world, if you have enough money, time, health, love, space, ripe avocados, motivation, orgasms, and will power — whatever — how would you want to feel?

I'm looking for feeling words, emotional states here. Write them down. Don't edit! Write down as many as you can think of, stream-of-consciousness style. Jotting without stopping.

How're you doing? Got a good start on the list? Great.

Now hang on to that list for a second.

If you don't have a list because you're not a spill-over-the-top word-lover like me, I'll direct you to a cheat sheet. Google

---

6   Danielle LaPorte, *The Firestarter Sessions: A Soulful & Practical Guide to Creating Success on Your Own Terms* (New York: Harmony Books, 2012), p 61.

"101 Core Desired Feelings," and a list by Ms. LaPorte will pop up.

Refer to that list, find the ones that make your heart rate speed up a bit, make you breathe a little easier, or just sound plain old attractive to you, and write those down! Those resonate with you.

How many words? I say start with about ten to fifteen, and then *whittle the list down to about five key words.*

Still struggling with the assignment? Okay, let me give you another way to come at this.

Close your eyes and imagine that you're early to your own surprise birthday party. The door to the party is slightly ajar, and just before you go walking in early and ruin the surprise everyone is trying to plan for you, you overhear the guests introducing themselves to each other:

"How do you know Katie?" "Did you guys work together?"

And you get to hear the answers:

"Oh we met on a cruise in 2016, and she convinced me to relax while snorkelling, and I had the best time," or "We worked together for years, and she always made the meetings more bearable; I adore her," or "Our dogs go to the same park, and she tells the funniest stories."

Point being, you are imagining what you'd be overhearing. The people are describing you in a happy, upbeat way, as they anticipate your joy at walking into a room full of your family and friends.

How are you described? Warm? Funny? Considerate? Resourceful? Organized? Powerful? Kind? A bit of a sarcastic dick? (*Oh dear, how did this person even get invited?*)

Do these words align with how you see yourself — with how you'd like to feel on a day-to-day basis? If they do,

write these words down. If these words are close, but not quite it, can you tweak them a little?

OK, so we have an idea of how we'd like to feel.

My own list goes something like this: joyful, confident, relaxed, playful, powerful and lit-up AF. And I want to feel this way every single day.

But I don't actually feel this way every day. I mean, I didn't. I do most of the time now, but I had to get myself organized and get rid of what wasn't working.

If you're on social media of any kind, it's pretty easy to see what other people are doing. I know a lot of the stuff on there is selective and filtered, but for the most part you can kind of tell if people are feeling good and like their lives, or if they're being petty and ranting about how the world has gone to hell in a handbasket. Let's take a moment to send the ranters some love, and then move on for the purpose of our work here.

When I first started this exercise a few years back, I found that while scrolling I was drawn to people who were running, walking their dogs, in business for themselves, stand-up paddleboarding, biking, snowshoeing, hiking, at the beach, in nature, preparing healthy food, and at the gym.

They were active, ate healthy food, and seemed to be happy creatives. They had what I wanted.

At this time, I also noticed that on the days when I sat around and ate poorly — basically anything that came packaged in bread and covered in cheese — I suffered from feelings of sadness, low motivation, lack of creativity, and plenty of anxiety.

Conversely, when I went to the gym, did yoga, watched my caffeine and sugar intake, walked the dog, and lined up a snowshoeing trek with my friends in the morning after a fresh snowfall, I felt the way I wanted to feel: happy, excited, creative, relaxed, playful, and strong.

This is easy math, friends. If you want to feel good more often, then move your body more often. I know you've heard the science behind this. During the first quarantine period of Covid-19 in early 2020, we all started going for more walks. Many of us did it because we had more time; but for most of us, after weeks of being indoors with nowhere to go, we needed to get out and see something different. I know I began to see more and more people walking. I saw struggling joggers who obviously thought, "I've got the time, so there's no excuse for not getting in shape now!" Yay, Human Spirit! I know that I had people join my online yoga classes who were completely new to the practice.

Instinctively, we knew that if we were going to survive this challenging time of uncertainty and fear with our mental health intact, then we needed to get out of our heads and into our bodies.

I'm going to go even a little further here, and hate me or not, this is the truth — not exercising daily is a form of self-sabotage. You are eroding the foundation of your potential skyscraper.

Remember that question at the beginning of the chapter: "How do you want to feel?"

Well, I guarantee that
out of shape,
low energy,
constipated,
fatigued,
depressed,
lonely,

and anxious
were not on anyone's list.

And yet, haven't we all experienced something similar as a direct result of too much time at the computer, or too much time on the couch?

Interestingly, after I did my research into what living as a happy person looked like, I began to make healthier food choices, which made me want to move my body more. And, when I'd lift weights at the gym or run five kilometres, I didn't dream of french fries; instead, I craved healthy food. Each activity was a boisterous cheering squad for the other.

LaPorte's original question kept returning to my mind when I'd get discouraged or return to old habits:

How do you want to *feel?*

How do you *want* to feel?

Well, I knew from experience that eating junk food regularly made me feel like a sad sack stuck on the shame train. I didn't want to feel like that.

I got interested in nutrition. I stopped ordering deep-fried food at restaurants. I ate the rainbow. My taste buds changed. As I gradually became more athletic and habitual in my nutritious lifestyle, I adopted a little mantra that ran through my mind each day: *I want to be vital. I want to feel full of vitality.*

While doing my original yoga-teacher training in 2013, I had the fortunate experience to live with a bunch of vegetarians for three weeks. During that time, I remember that I ate chicken and a tuna steak once. I experienced a huge revelation that I felt spectacular when I didn't eat animal products. Now, I'm not telling you to give up meat here. That was my personal experience only. I urge you to find out what works best for you to support your goals.

I'm sure you're wondering about how vegetarians get enough daily protein because I'm still asked this question frequently. Our North American society is obsessed with this; we have been taught that a high-protein, low-carb diet is the ticket to dietary success. First of all, there are a myriad of plant-based protein sources available, so don't worry, I'm not breaking down into a frail old lady anytime soon. Secondly, studies have shown that those living in the world's Blue Zones — areas where they have the most centenarians (people who live to be 100 years old or more) actually eat a LOW-protein diet. A low-protein diet had been proved to be a key contributor to their longevity. Point being: there are many ways to live and to eat, and you have to find out what works best for you.

The goal, regardless of what you choose, is to stay focused on how you want to feel every day, on that embodied experience we crave. This is another step in creating a life of freedom and joy. There's a crucial caveat to this lesson however: eating well and exercising more should never be done in a self-punishing way.

If you angrily choke down a green smoothie for breakfast all the while resenting that it's not a Denny's Super Slam, I'm not sure how much that is helping you or healing you.

Do you complain and groan constantly before, during, and after your workouts? Isn't that a confusing message you're sending to a body that is trying to eliminate free radicals, build muscle, burn fat, and support your cellular structure?

And what about vibrational energy? We've already established that this is a thing. It's like one hand keeps building a Jenga tower, and the other hand keeps pulling out the base blocks and compromising the integrity of the structure.

Or quite simply put, are you eating and exercising from a place of lack, or one of sufficiency, joy, and abundance?

Allow me to share with you another mind-blowing moment that truly drives home this truth. Our minds cannot be well if our bodies are not, and vice versa. I received this wisdom from a quiet, understated, emergency-room doctor who is also well-versed in Traditional Chinese Medicine.

On another yoga teacher training in Santa Cruz, California, a group of us piled into the local hotspot on a lunch break.

Ordering a meal in a restaurant with a group of yoga teachers is one of the most comical things you'll witness. One person asks for gluten-free; a couple are strict vegans and want to be sure there's no dairy or animal products of any kind in the food.

Someone else asks, *Is there lard in the bread?*

Are the vegetables local and organic?

You get the picture. We are a slightly high-strung, high-maintenance group.

I'm sitting beside John* this amazing wise doctor, and he orders off the menu without asking the waitress one question. I kind of smile and look at him quizzically as she takes our menus away from the table. His lack of concern as to what he would be receiving was decidedly noticeable in the present company.

I'll never forget what he said, in his soft reassuring voice:

"The anxiety that we feel about the food we are consuming may in fact inhibit our body's ability to fully absorb the

nutrients from that food. To get the most nutritional value, perhaps we should eat without worry."

I almost cried.

I mean, for years every single thing I ate came with a mental scan of whether it was high in fat, high in carbs, high in sugar, known to cause cancer, would expand my carbon footprint, was dripping with pesticides, harmed any animals in its production, was politically correct, regionally significant, was dishonouring the tradition of those who originally created it, was full of refined flour, was under my points for the day, and so on.

Does any of this sound familiar to you?

I mean, sheesh. How is our body, our beautiful, magnificent body, supposed to function optimally when scrambled by these love–hate messages as we try to feed it?

Some decisions are like flicking a light switch. Others are more gradual, like the green summer leaves fading to brown in the fall. I can't say how things will happen for you. In my case, from that moment on, in the company of a man I've never dined with since, I stopped worrying about everything else, and allowed myself to be fed.

I'm suggesting that you breathe into your body, nourish your body, forgive your body, and send messages of love to your body, daily.

I like to say, *Just stop, and just start.*

Just stop focusing on your shortcomings.

Just start focusing on what is working.

Just stop regarding your body with a measuring tape in one hand and a magazine cover in the other.

Just start counting your physical gifts.

And now to be perfectly honest, and forgiving, and FULL of love, I want to remind you that transitions can be a series of two steps forward and one step back. No story is a straight line, and progress is not a consistent chronological climb upward, ever.

Yes, there will be days.

There have been days when this plucky, polite, sunny girl couldn't wait to slam things around at the gym, lift heavy, push, pull, sweat, grunt, gasp for breath, and not worry about the expression on her face, you know? And there's nothing wrong when I get like that either. It's just that we can't always be one thing. And we shouldn't have to be.

We are three-dimensional creatures, so we should be able to experience the full range of human emotion too. We are all a work in progress. We are all struggling and succeeding simultaneously.

Let's not hide.
We are worthy, just as we are.
Baby steps, and big gratitude.
Every damn day.

And to the gents out there who feel that they always have to be strong, have it all together, and know all of the answers, I'm here to tell you that it's totally fine if you don't.

It's actually normal to feel

sad,

scared,

tired,

lonely

and indecisive, too.

Let's all be human and start from there. It's a worthy journey. And bring your suitcase with you.

PUTTING IN THE WORK AGAIN: THE BIG F***ING LIST OF WHAT YOU WANT

In a separate part of your journal, start writing a numbered list of what you want. This can include everything from a house on the water, to a vintage Jaguar, to an organic smoothie delivery service, to a chihuahua. (*Oh wait, this sounds a lot like my list!*)

Anyway, NO CENSORING, just keep writing it all down.

Put down every single thing you want to own, do and experience. Add to this list every time something pops into your head. You will find that:

(a) you will start to receive/manifest/create opportunities for these items to come into being, and

(b) you don't want that much actual "stuff" after all.

You want experiences, and you want to feel a certain way. But it's a cool exercise. Have fun with it and let your imagination run wild!

HEY, RADAR

The magic
began
when
she shut off the TV,
closed all the books,
and tuned in
to herself.

CHAPTER 5:
IT'S ALL YOU, BABY: MIND, BODY, SPIRIT — AND YOU'VE GOTTA BELIEVE IT'S NOT BROKEN

There was a time when I taught yoga classes as exercise. And as all good yoginis should, I soon realized what I was actually doing was creating a space for people to self-heal. As I've previously mentioned, so much of this understanding for me started with that wise-cracking and wise Texan, Brené Brown.

I was innocently navigating my way to personal self-improvement by accepting my flaws, while immersed in Brown's *The Gifts of Imperfection: Let Go of Who You Think You're Supposed to Be and Embrace Who You Are*[7] when she quoted another writer, Lynne Twist, from *her* book called *The Soul of Money: Reclaiming the Wealth of Our Inner Resources.*[8]

As I've mentioned earlier, I was introduced to the concept of a **sufficiency** versus a **scarcity** mindset, and my mind was cracked wide open, never to be reformed in the same way again. So much so that I had to buy all new hats.

What I didn't expect however, was that if I applied this concept to sharing yoga with others and creating a space of

7 Brown, *The Gifts of Imperfection*, p. 82–84.
8 Twist, *The Soul of Money*.

complete acceptance and love, then people would begin to heal physically, emotionally, and spiritually. I'm telling you; I've seen it happen again and again.

Over the years, I have received hundreds of thank-you notes from my students, who couldn't quite put their finger on what was different about doing yoga with me, but they felt better.

Of course, none of this would have been possible if I wasn't the student first. If I didn't slog through my own waters of poor self-worth and negative body image and get to the other side.

In that one remarkably powerful paragraph of her book, Twist set this process in motion for me. According to Twist, it's thoughts of lack generated unconsciously that constantly leave us feeling a sense of lack. We always feel like we're behind, we're missing out, and we're not enough. One of the main lines in particular that was the catalyst for the change in my thinking was this one. I can't tell you how many times I've re-read it:[9]

> This mantra of *not enough* carries the day and becomes a kind of default setting for our thinking about everything, from the cash in our pocket to the people we love or the value of our own lives. What begins as a simple expression of the hurried life, or even the challenged life, grows into the great justification for an unfulfilled life.

Mic drop.

I have paraphrased the heck out of both Brown's and Twist's books here, and I *highly* recommend reading everything they've

---

9   Twist, *The Soul of Money*, p. 44

written, but the point is, I got the full-body shivers when I read this.

It reminded me that although I was basically a joyful person, I was still dealing with feelings of unworthiness. But I also began to feel just a tiny bit unstuck. *And* curious about how to put this into practice as a yoga teacher and shift more folks towards joy, if I could.

I would read this paragraph and a few others in class to share this perspective. As I read the book cover to cover, I realized that, yes, I had indeed been focusing the first forty-five-plus years of my life on what I didn't have. I thought that was simply having goals. I thought I was always supposed to want more.

I, like everyone else, was simply focused on the hustle, and I didn't realize that I was also unwittingly feeding my own insecurities in doing so. For the first time, I understood that if I was constantly pursuing *other*, then I would never feel good about where I *was*.

This new focus translated very well for me as a teacher. I had previously designed my flow class sequences to challenge my students and bring them to their "edge" physically. Maybe the breathing felt good and the music carried us along, but many, including myself, likely ended the class without opening up their mind–soul freeways.

I began to joke around in class more. I craved lightness. I wanted to promote a sense of sufficiency, so I stuck with easier, feel-good poses that most bodies found accessible. I called them "confidence builders." Remarkably, my students' mind-sets toward their bodies, their abilities, and their practice on the mat changed before my eyes.

I kept encouraging them to see their bodies from a place of sufficiency.

I'd say, "Simply notice what you can do." And miraculously they did a little more and a little more, and they also kept coming to class.

ANNA'S STORY

One student in particular, Anna,* would return to me week after week, exclaiming how she was continually feeling better coming to see me even though she "couldn't quite explain it." On the phone before our first private session, Anna told me about chronic pain in her hip, discomfort due to scoliosis, and her struggles with anxiety and depression.

That first day, she entered my private studio tentatively and exhausted. We worked on breathing, did a few restorative poses, and I asked her for feedback throughout, explaining that it was my job to add and remove props until she was comfortable. Anna cried with relief during the session and other times, too, because we had managed to alleviate her pain temporarily.

Accepting her progress as it came, I did not reinforce the tapes playing in her head. They said that she was too old, too damaged, and in too much pain to ever have fun again. It broke my heart as she expressed shame about her lack of self-care and poor lifestyle choices that had possibly exacerbated her current medical conditions.

I was certainly not qualified to comment on her situation medically.

Instead, I simply encouraged her.

I remarked on how responsive she was to the breathing techniques and the restorative practice, how I could sense her growing more relaxed and lessening her grip on her painful areas. How her range of motion improved. How she was settling into meditations more quickly and recognizing which props suited her body best.

I had also noticed that when Anna first started with me, she was constantly apologizing.

She was sorry for coming too early, sorry for not understanding my cues the first time, sorry for needing a particular prop removed, sorry that she couldn't do more. Again, I'm no psychologist, but I believed that focusing on what was lacking was not going to move her forward. Instead, I came up with an assignment for her.

Her assignment between sessions was to record with little ticks on a piece of paper how many times she apologized in one day. She laughed in embarrassment when she told me her count the first time. But gradually, those ticks became less.

After a year and a half, Anna went from being bent over and in chronic pain to a happier being, with her face lifted. She laughed at herself and apologized less often. She bought herself a bicycle and rode for the first time in years. On the days when she overdid it and the pain returned, she would give herself rest, practising some breathing techniques to keep the worry in check. Anna's confidence grew.

When her belief in her health strengthened, it seemed that her pain lessened.

My sessions with Anna certainly reinforced my instincts about my students' ability to heal, but when fifteen-year-old Jenny* showed up on my doorstep, my mindset changed forever.

Indulge me here as I tell another story, because I think it's important and may help you on the path to understanding your own approach to loving and ultimately healing your lovely self.

I had known Jenny since she was a baby. We lived in the same small town and my path crossed frequently with her mother's. There was a fondness between us moms, but as lives go, we were both too busy to connect socially.

So, imagine how upset I was when Jenny's mother called me up in tears one day to tell me that the girl I remembered as a carefree, big-eyed toddler had been suffering in pain for months. And just that day, Jenny had been diagnosed with scoliosis. I knew that Jenny had always been active in organized sports; she played both soccer and volleyball on rep teams.

More x-rays were needed in order to get a better diagnosis and treatment plan, "but is there anything I can do to help her right now?" her mom asked hopefully.

The old me would have been discouraging. I would have said, "It's best to see what the doctors say."

But I was distraught at the thought of Jenny, confused and in a whole heap of pain.

I had also expanded my approach on how to use yoga poses, philosophy, breath work, and meditation. Experience was revealing these to me as powerful and tangible tools to stoke the innate confidence in our beings.

That experience was showing me how my students could shift the experience of pain in their bodies.

I told her mother that there were two things I could offer:

I could show Jenny how to manage the fear of her pain by using breathing techniques.

And I could teach her how to use props to temporarily alleviate a bit of the discomfort.

That was it.

Jenny spent a total of eight one-hour sessions with me. She was a fast learner, and in that short period of time I observed that she went from feeling scared and powerless over her scoliosis diagnosis to secure in a system of personal pain management. In our sessions, we experimented with breathing, props, restorative yoga postures, visualizations and meditations, and a fabulous tool developed by American physiotherapist Jill Miller called the Coregeous Ball.* (See www.tuneupfitness.com for more information on this.)

I encouraged Jenny the whole time, saying how rapidly she was learning the techniques, how well she knew her own body and listened to its responses, and how powerful her mind was. I constantly asked for her feedback and took a lot of notes. I made it clear from the outset that Jenny was in the driver's seat as far as these sessions went. All of my ideas were suggestions, but her feedback would decide the direction we would go.

We chatted softly throughout our sessions and covered a lot of topics: teenage concerns about competitive girls and clueless Grade 8 boys — but we laughed a lot, too.

I encouraged, I encouraged, I encouraged. Truthfully, I can't say that I did much else.

My studio space has low lighting, quiet music, and a cute little electric fireplace. It was a soft place to land for someone like Jenny who was always striving to do her best and used reinforcement from the outside world as the only way to gauge if she was succeeding at life.

For my part, I wanted this girl to see how much she had, how much we *all* have. And when her pain was eased, she felt this, I know. On the day of her last session, tears were shed by Jenny, her mom, and me. I would be available for check-ins if needed, but Jenny felt confident that she could still play sports, handle what the doctors had to say, and use the techniques she had learned to keep her pain in check. It was a moving experience for all of us to witness how this girl's self-assurance had grown.

From that point on, a new approach to clients was born. I'd always start with what was working, see what we could do, and go from there. My clients would invariably leave feeling better. Over time, they'd develop confidence in their bodies again, which sometimes I'd witness spilling over into other areas of their lives.

I can't even express with words how much clients like Jenny and Anna changed me; taught me. And it didn't take me long to recognize that practically everyone I met needed a little nudge, a little love, in order to see themselves through a slightly softer lens, myself included. We also greatly needed to yoke our minds to our bodies that we'd somehow become so disassociated from.

At the time of this writing, I only occasionally teach yoga or work with clients in chronic pain. Life has surprised me yet again with requests to apply this philosophy to personal performance coaching, and now book writing coaching.

I will always love yoga. It's calm and slow. And it's kind of ridiculous sometimes, too — the way we bend, and put our bums up in the air in snug pants. Those aspects appeal to the goofball in me.

In fact, sometimes I'd joke with my students about what would be on my T-shirts if I'd designed a line of yoga-related clothing.

I've only got eyes for your pelvis.
I'm all about your organs.
Breathe into the space between your toes.
Ha, ha; say what?

All jokes aside, as a yoga teacher, a mother, an author, a coach, and friend, I only have two messages that I want to spread. And they are so simple, but need to be heard:

"You. You are whole just as you are. There's nothing wrong with you."
"Just begin and pour a heap of love on yourself along the way."

That's it.

Love yourself as you are now, because you are already whole. If you want to change, or grow, or learn, or develop, you can do that. We can all do that. But don't do it from a place of desperation and shame, but instead from a place of:

"It's all good here; I just want to move in a slightly different direction that will make the good stuff even better."

I can share this with conviction because I needed to learn it the most.

You see, for years I was racing around, always busy, striving with my veins popping, not truly connected to my heart, to what was happening in my body or, most importantly, to the messages of my soul. And in order to live joyfully and

to our highest purpose, we must learn to put on the breaks. Just stop, and just start again.

In her book, *Present Over Perfect: Leaving Behind Frantic for a Simpler, More Soulful Way of Living,* Shauna Niequist created the most accurate snapshot of me as a young mom: bombing around in a snack-packed minivan, transporting my three kids from intellectually–emotionally–spiritually–athletically–socially–stimulating activity to activity, squeezing in teaching, sex with my husband, and still always arriving with a meticulously-wrapped gift at every family function:

> My regrets: how many years I bruised people with my fragmented, anxious presence. How many moments of connection I missed — too busy, too tired, too frantic and strung out on the drug of efficiency.
>
> Now I know there's another way.
>
> You don't have to damage your body and your soul and the people you love most in order to get done what you think you have to get done.
>
> You don't have to live like this.[10]

Do you relate to that too?

For my part, I had been living as a Hummer who rolled right over the slower cars; I was a snow plow who clipped mailboxes along my route, careless of the breadth of my blade, with the interior of my vehicle littered with receipts and drips of

---

10   Shauna Niequist, *Present Over Perfect: Leaving Behind Frantic for a Simpler, More Soulful Way of Living* (Grand Rapids: Zondervan, 2016), p. 28.

spilled coffee, as I rushed at a breakneck speed, to give everyone everything I thought they wanted.

Heck, for years I lived with a shoulder that chronically dislocated due to an injury that occurred when I was eighteen, stoically accepting the trips to the ER to put it back in place as another chore on my to-do list. I was too busy to take myself to the doctor and attend to it properly.

Does this sound familiar to you? Have you been ignoring a condition in your body, an ache, a heaviness, a sadness even, because you are too caught up in anxious striving?

That's OK. We've all done it.

But you don't have to keep that up, and you are not alone.

Learn to pause and identify what you need. This is how we learn to believe that we are enough, one breath at a time.

PUTTING IN THE WORK: VALUING YOUR BODY

Get calm. Get clear. Move forward with joy.

This is a big one, Friends, and it starts with the most accessible and potent tool we have. This tool is portable, costs absolutely nothing, and is right under our noses.

It is our breath.

There is no quicker way to calm us down or fire us up, than to deliberately breathe more slowly or more quickly. Long, slow, and wide inhalations and exhalations slow down our heart rate, lower our blood pressure, reduce levels of cortisol and adrenalin being dumped into our systems, and help us see more clearly.

Conversely, speeding up our breathing for a short period of time may give us an energetic burst. I will address creating an energetic burst at another time. For now, we are going to focus on growing quiet and calming our central nervous systems, so that we can truly listen to what our bodies are saying to us. This is how we learn to recognize if we are hungry, tired, what emotions are predominant at that time, and if we are experiencing discomfort anywhere.

Let your body talk to you. Learn to grow quiet and still often. Remember, it's all you, from head to toe, from innermost cell to every eyelash, and it's all of cherished worth.

Just pause.

Sit upright wherever you are and close your eyes, or at least lower your gaze, and allow your eyes to be soft as they tip towards your heart.

Inhale through your nose and sigh your breath out of your mouth. Repeat again.

Now, place your hands on your ribs with your middle fingers touching. Inhale slowly through your mouth and notice that your middle fingers are pulled apart ever so slightly. Exhale and your middle fingers touch again. Repeat this three to five times. Have you noticed that your breathing has already slowed down? If not, start again. When ready, move on to the next part.

Rest your hands in your lap, or down by your sides, whichever is more comfortable. Eyes closed or lowered again, take a long, slow, deep and wide breath in through your nose, lifting and expanding the chest, the ribs, the sides of you, and the back, while doing so. Then, exhale through your nose, making each inhale and exhale a bit longer, until you find the best rhythm for you. The goal is to be slow and steady. If you feel your heart rate speeding up, you're trying too hard. Take it easy. Just let it happen.

Ok, now we're going to count the breath. When you inhale this time, count how many beats it takes. Don't push it. Count the beats on your exhale. Do this again.

Now, choose a comfortable length for the count of the inhale and make the exhalation count longer by two beats. So, for example, if you inhale to the count of six, you'll exhale to the count of eight. Continue this pattern for three to five breaths.

Then sit comfortably, gaze soft or eyes closed.

It's now time to notice what is going on in your body.

Do a little scan of your whole being. Is there a wrist or a knee that is sore? Do you have tension in your neck or upper back? And what emotional state are you in right now? Simply notice and accept; don't be in a hurry to trade a "negative" emotion for a "positive" one. Sometimes we are angry or sad, and that is OK.

This exercise is so valuable, because we are getting into the feel of our bodies and our emotional state from a place of non-judgment. We are not rushing to the area, lights flashing, sirens blaring, to fix, fix, fix, or save ourselves. This is a practice of observing and getting comfortable with what is.

As we become more experienced with this, we become more attuned to what our bodies need — rest, an ice pack, movement, water, massage, strengthening, love — so that we can feel good inside of our remarkable vibrational home.

Over time, we come to recognize that our emotions and our identity are not the same. While sitting and breathing we may observe, "Oh there is some worry here," or "There is some disappointment or grief there."

These are simply experiences we are having, not just in our minds but also carried in our physical bodies, that through love, acceptance, and rest, we may eventually be able to release.

Some of you may wish to journal about what you observe during these quiet times. Go ahead if that feels right to you. If you have a trusted member of your healthcare team, you could even share with that person what you've observed is going on.

Remember though — you are not broken.

You are not a vehicle to be taken into the mechanic and disassembled into parts and repaired. You are already whole, just as you are.

If anything, think of yourself as a plant that you want to make sure gets lots of sun, and you play soft R&B music to. The more that you listen to your body and tend to it with water, nourishment, rest, and encouragement, the healthier and more joyful you will be.

A SON CALLED LION

I have a son I call Lion.
I remember him so small,
Standing on his toes,
flashing his eyes
at a man who called him Little.
Lion roars
thrashes
protects
any and all the triflings.
I stand with pride and awe,
then remember that he is made
of pieces of me
and so I must be a Lion, too.

CHAPTER 6:
LEARNING TO CATCH

When I was in university, I had this roommate named Roxy*.

Roxy was in a music and theatre program, so she was always in dance clothes and reciting lines dramatically, and I was in what I deemed to be a "very serious" journalism program.

Subsequently, we had quite different lifestyles, different friends, and kept different hours. Roxy would get up early to go clean a local dance studio in exchange for free dance classes. I would sleep-in, have a couple cups of coffee, and drag myself to class in a slightly disgruntled and skeptical fashion. I imagined real journalists would do likewise.

One evening as I was working on homework and drinking Diet Coke, the doorbell rang. Some good-looking guy I didn't know was dropping off chicken wings and a salad for Roxy, who wouldn't be home for another hour.

The next morning, I heard a car idling outside of the house. Someone else was there waiting to drive Roxy to the dance studio for 6 a.m. Often, another friend would drive her home at night. This all sounds rather circumspect, doesn't it? However, I'll tell you that I overheard her on the phone one night with one of these friends and found out why everyone was showing up for her.

She was literally ASKING FOR HELP — a drive some-where if it wasn't out of their way, or a Tupperware of some soup that they'd made themselves for dinner and had extras of anyway.

I was aghast! What kind of strong, independent woman would ask for a ride somewhere?

One who arrived at school with dry boots and hair and eye-lashes that had not frozen on the walk there, that's who!

It didn't take me long to notice that my roommate had help all around her. Knowing how hard she worked, her friends wanted to help her out. And she was always appreciative. She said thank you, or would squeal, "You're the best!" when yet another treat was dropped off for her.

I was both disgusted and confused by the help Roxy was asking for and receiving. True to my roots as a Canadian pioneer woman from three generations back, I valued inde-pendence highly. I considered my ability to struggle as a badge of honour. That demonstrated my superiority as I took care of my own business, didn't it?

But let me tell you something: I was tired. I was tired all the time of overseeing my own transportation, my own meals, my studies, and keeping my own counsel. Roxy, on the other hand, seemed to be gliding through these super-long days with a smile on her face, a sense of joy, and good company.

She was doing something that I never imagined myself doing; she was asking for help.

I don't know about you, but I had always been raised with independence as one of the strongest values. Asking for help, especially as a woman, was considered a sign of weakness. But I'll tell you, when I compared my days of trudging back and forth to school, scrambling to find something to eat at the last minute, to Roxy, who was surrounded by friends, and had support and great companionship, I gave it a real hard thought. These people seem genuinely delighted to do things for her! I had to be missing something, I thought, as I reached for my bowl of tomato soup in the stubborn solitude of my university bedroom.

I wish I could say that I learned the lesson back then, but I did not. The epiphany came many years later after I was married and had three children. And I'm not the only one who took some time to learn this one.

I heard famed motivational speaker and transformational coach, Tony Robbins, on The Maria Forleo Podcast this year, how he had to learn to catch himself, too. Robbins grew up poor, so when he started to experience success as a young man, he always picked up the cheque every time he had lunch or dinner with work colleagues or friends. As Robbins himself tells it, this soon became a well-communicated fact, and he attracted some people to him who were there simply for the free meal. He had to distinguish the true supporters from the freeloaders the hard way. Despite this, however, he continued to pay for meals because it made him feel so good to take care of others, be generous, and treat them to something special.

A few years into his successful coaching career, one of the mentors and business leaders Robbins truly admired made time to dine with him. The meeting went well and, as per usual, Robbins reached for the cheque. He was astonished by the sharp sting of pain he felt as this man slapped him hard on the hand as he reached for it. He pulled his hand away in shock and embarrassment, raising his face in search of an explanation.

The mentor said to Robbins, "After our lovely dinner and this special time together, how dare you insult me, in fact, rob me of the pleasure of buying *you* this meal?"

Robbins is a smart guy and quickly came to understand that he had been standing up there on the pitching mound alone for a very long time. He learned from his mentor that true leadership involves allowing others a chance to lead. Essentially, he learned to catch; he learned to receive.

The light didn't truly turn on for me until many years later, when I stumbled across this incredible meditation, seemingly written specifically for me. It was called, "Become a Better Receiver."

I read it and got chills. And wow, I figured out what had happened twenty some years ago, living with Roxy.

This meditation outlined the pleasure we get if we're always the Giver. How we want to keep on giving gifts, dropping off surprise meals, popping pretty cards in the mail "just because," and generally take care of others because we want to keep on feeling those good feelings that we get from giving.

We feel generous.

We feel joy in our ability to deliver tangible gifts.

We feel pleasure from draping our love all over another person.

We feel organized, powerful, thoughtful, and maybe even just a tiny bit magnanimous when we give.

This unforgettable meditation used the analogy of a baseball pitcher throwing a ball to a catcher:

How is the baseball pitcher supposed to improve if the catcher isn't there?

Let's take this analogy to our relationships. If you are always the pitcher and never the catcher, then how does anyone else improve their fastball, their curve, their change-up? How do they get better at the giving and, subsequently, the loving?

In order to allow others to get better at demonstrating love, giving love, and being creative with finding ways of

demonstrating love, then we have to be the receiver. We have to catch the ball.

Otherwise, it could also be said that we're being selfish. We don't give others the opportunity to experience the same pleasure we did as the Giver. We must sometimes be the Receiver in order to be a good cosmic dance partner. We need to receive gifts of love, time, favours, meals, drives to places, and compliments.

I tell you; I see this all the time with my female friends. I'm going over to a friend's house, and I'm not allowed to bring anything. She has all the food organized. She has the place decorated; she has a signature cocktail ready. She just wants me to show up. Meanwhile, when I arrive, oftentimes my hostess looks harried and exhausted or even just a touch resentful.

Here's another example. As parents, we do the same thing. We want to do everything for our children. As a result, they don't learn how to do things for others. They simply haven't had the practice. Have you ever had a birthday roll around, and your kids have done virtually nothing for you? We think that we're teaching them how to throw a good birthday party by throwing them amazing ones. But if we're never allowing them to have the actual practice of organizing the guest list, wrapping the gifts, plating the appetizers, and icing the cake, we impede their ability to give.

In order to have rich relationships, we must gracefully ask for and accept help from others.

Not with guilt or apologies.

Not with the fear that we look weak or incapable. We must quell the immediate compulsion to reciprocate.

We also don't always have to be the one spreading money around on an outing. Sometimes we can leave our fierce

pride in our wallets. Allow someone else the opportunity to feel the sense of satisfaction that comes from treating a friend.

As a partner in parenting, did you feel the compulsion to do everything for your babies when they were little? Perhaps you wouldn't let your partner do the diapering, bathing, dressing the baby, or packing the diaper bag, because you wanted to do it all. And so you kept him/her outside of those moments. They never had the opportunity to get their hands dirty and experience that level of love for the child. I'm sorry if that hurts, but you're not alone. I know that's exactly what I did. I gobbled up all that time and attention with each of my children, secretly gloating a little about how my babies always reached for me first.

We need to think about where this comes from if we're going to make a change.

Perhaps it stems from insecurity (*I'm going to be the best Mom ever!*) or maybe it comes from that socially ingrained codependency, and the universal need to please. We are told from girlhood that women are nurturers, anthropologically speaking. How many women in their twenties and thirties get asked when they are going to start a family? We are supposed to be nice girls, and nice girls take care of others, and motherhood is the perfect opportunity to glorify our "naturally occurring" unselfishness. Sheesh. I don't know about you, but that's not the only quality I've got. And had I actually shared the load and allowed others to work their magic, I might not have been exhausted and resentful at times.

If you're still running yourself ragged, racing against the clock, and you're driven by this constant desire for perfection, then guess what, my friend?

You need to learn to catch the ball.

And let somebody else throw it for a change.

Let somebody else be up on that pitching mound showing what they can do. Why does it always have to be you?

This is powerful stuff. I know that sometimes it takes more time to show someone else how to do things. It's faster to do things yourself, you tell yourself. Oh, geez. Let's rethink these excuses cobbled together by the ego and think ahead to the future of your relationships.

Are you able to let go of the ball and give someone else a chance to get in there?

Are you able to receive, thereby freeing others to demonstrate their love?

The way others do things might not be exactly the way you do it, and it might not be done as quickly, as efficiently or economically, but step back anyway. Ask for help. Allow others to learn, and you might learn some things yourself, too. Allow others to grow their skills.

And stop wearing yourself out. By asking others for help, you give yourself some mental and physical wiggle room. What would happen if you had a little bit of time to sit and reflect, even journal? Go for a walk? Have a nap? Instead of always being the smartest person in the room, always being the engine that runs your corner of the world, step back and give someone else a chance to shine.

Remember that every time you ask someone for help, you are giving that person a gift. You are giving them an opportunity to learn, grow, and practise loving.

PUTTING IN THE WORK:
CULTIVATING AWARENESS

The first step in becoming a Receiver is awareness. Studies have shown that as soon as we become aware of certain behaviours, we have already begun to change them.

Take the time to journal on these questions and observations:

1. Do you allow others the opportunity to give, or do you always have to be the Giver?
2. List all the ways that you receive help or allow others to take care of you.
3. Where can you do more of this; even receive from your children?
4. How does being the receiver challenge your own view of yourself?
5. Observe how your relationships change.

After completing the above, send me a private message on Instagram @marcybeyourself. This is fascinating stuff to me. If you commit to this, I guarantee your personal relationships will change for the better.

DAMN EASY

I've been a handful.
I am a handful
and I wish I was different
I always have wished
that I was docile, patient, quiet.
But then the noise starts to bubble up
from the inside,
bursting
the damn of easy.
There's nothing easy about me.
I care too much,
squeeze too much in,
wake up woke
everyday.
Who can keep that pace?
No one
and maybe no one else should be
riding this
exhilarating wave —
bursting the damn
of easy.

CHAPTER 7:
THE LION TAMER VS. THE OPEN-ARMED MAMA

Remember that I told you that I would address the fact that I talked a lot as a kid and why that's significant to this book?

Well, my mother did a spectacular job of keeping grade school photo albums for us as kids, complete with all the school awards and class pictures from each grade. I loved this book. I loved looking at how my friends and I had changed from year to year and laughing at the clothes that were the must-haves at the time.

One trip home years ago on a break from university, I pulled that album from my mother's shelf. I devoured the long-forgotten report cards. Maybe I needed to boost my confidence with midterm exams fast approaching.

Despite some drama with other girls, I had loved grade school and remembered it as a good experience. Yet as I opened the report cards from each year's sleeve and read them, I felt myself fall into that old familiar pit of shame. Year after year, almost every teacher remarked that although they appreciated my enthusiasm, they also commented on how much I had to say:

"Marcy is an excellent student, but it would be nice if she'd allow others to answer the questions sometimes." Or, "If Marcy would be just a bit quieter; it might be easier for others around her to learn."

My fanciful trip down memory lane ended with me wading through old fears that lived in the pit of my stomach, home of my deepest secret: I was somehow not as awesome as I thought I was. There was something wrong with me!

Had I been that noisy? Was I unbearable? I know that my grandmother always sighed as I plopped down on the couch ungracefully as a young person, and my mom to this day still rolls her eyes as I share, "yet another long story."

Despite experiences like this, I remember simply being just so darn excited about life. On the inside, I felt like I was bounding into a room, eager to make people laugh with my storytelling, often highlighting my own blunders. I knew I was flawed but felt confident in the knowledge that so was everyone else. No one had taught me that; I'd always just sensed that and loved the humanity in it.

I remember my Grade 4 friends sitting around me in snow banks amphitheatre-style at recess begging me to re-enact skits from *The Carol Burnett Show*. I loved to read aloud or get up in front of the class. I talked to everybody, because heck, everyone was so darn interesting to me. People were a veritable treasure trove of quirky family routines, hush-hush crushes, favourite foods, and even how-to instructions on managing different hair textures.

As I got a little older, I continued to use my self-deprecating humour to make others feel comfortable enough around me to open up about their own hopes, dreams and fears *(Look at me, I'm a goofball! I make mistakes! You can tell me anything!)*. I mean, yes, sometimes the shy people would go running, but I was exactly where I wanted to be all the time — surrounded by beautiful humans.

Despite my bravado, however, all of the years of shushing did take a toll on me. Deep down, I wished that I could be quiet and still and full of grace. I became self-conscious of my loud laughter. I tried to trim the length of what I had to say.

I hustled hard in all that I did, graduating university with a high GPA. In every early professional role I had, I tucked my big personality into pencil skirts and blazers, praying that I could dodge the familiar comments about how chatty I was that I'd heard for so long.

I'm telling this story because I know that I'm not alone in this experience. It's part of the human condition to want to conform for fear that we do not fit in because, historically speaking, those who are "different" are often cast out of the tribe.

Haven't we evolved past that though? Or shouldn't we? I was so confused by the messages I'd been given to date. One message told me to "go for it", and other ones told me to "act like a lady" and hem myself in. I was perpetually confused as to where the imaginary borders lie between the two.

I ask you, why do the loud people need to grow quiet, and the quiet ones need to come out of their shells? Who decided that it all runs better when we're all the same? Who wants to be "moderate" anyway? OK, OK, I'm not calling for chaos here.

I am talking about crushing spirits and creating shame. I'm concerned about the comments and criticisms that carelessly toss countless beings into the pit of "not enough." The ones that feed the culture of lack and make us stop trusting those voices deep inside.

We've all been told that we're either too loud or too shy.

That we need leadership skills, or we need to settle down.

We need to grow some balls. We need to slow down and take a moment and think.

We need to man up, or we need to back off and let others have a chance.

Oh, my.

So many messages have been delivered to so many people who are treated as if they came into this world as fragmented sections of a whole. Let's stop treating others as though they need moulding, repairing, re-shaping and re-programming if they're going to survive.

This world is not one size fits all.

I thought the goal in life was to be the Youest You you could ever be.

In his half novel, half treatise, *Emile*, Eighteenth-century philosopher Jean-Jacques Rousseau shared the original outlook that children are not empty vessels that need filling up. Instead they are full of natural gifts who simply require the time, freedom, and space to reveal their true, natural personalities. Rousseau's outlook ties into the way that we see ourselves, and whether we are operating from a place of sufficiency or scarcity.

I can't stop people from saying unkind things, and neither can you. So, here's where your sense of personal responsibility kicks in again.

Dig deep. Get to know yourself. Or as Dr. Nicole LePera says, *Do the work.*

The messages that you deliver to yourself on a consistent daily basis are more powerful than all of the awful things that were ever said to you throughout your lifetime. And it is your responsibility to heal.

When you are playing the piano, making pasta by hand, taking a course at work, or learning Thai massage, how do you talk to yourself? Do you work under the assumption that you're a screw-up and you've just gotta make this work — you've just got to succeed? Or are you gentle and patient with yourself any time you try something new?

Learning is a vulnerable state to be in.

So, I encourage you to speak softly to yourself, whispering encouragement, and forgiving little mistakes the way an open-armed Mama would, instead of pushing through the experience desperate and afraid that if you fail, you'll feel the whip of a lion tamer.

How do you treat yourself when you are unsure?

Indeed, the spirit with which we do something is dramatically more significant to our personal well-being than what is actually getting done. It's tough to learn in an environment wrought with fear, one that begins and ends with the supposition that we are not enough.

We must learn to love our frailties and develop that inner confidence that acts like a giant Teflon F-U shield in the face of criticism. The way I see it, someone will always not get our vibe, but on the other hand, someone will always love us, too.

It took me a long time to accept and understand that I'd always be a big talker. I was nervous as a cat for a long time and haunted by my limiting belief that "I was just a little too much." I felt everything so intensely, including the disapproval of those who were uncomfortable with my boisterous disposition and fearless conversations.

Thankfully, as the saying goes: *my mess became my message.*

I knew that I thrived on connection with others but also realized that my natural tendency to take up a lot of space could sometimes make others feel as though they were not heard. I didn't need to dismantle my effusive nature, but I needed to grow some complementary skills. Do you see the difference in the self-talk, the basis of the assumption here?

I'm allowing myself the hug from the open-armed Mama instead of fearfully running from the whip of the lion tamer.

In my case, the lifeblood of a talker is having a good listener. And in order to have a good listener who sticks around, I had to learn to become one myself. Not only did I learn that the more articulate you are, the more responsible you are for the impact of the words you so easily string together. I also learned that if I'm going to expect others to listen to me, then I needed to close my lips and reciprocate the focus on them.

What a lesson.

These days, there's nothing I love more than a good, deep and wide conversation, where we take things apart and try to understand our motives, acknowledge our shortcomings, and sort it all in an embrace of love. I am blessed with rich friendships, some more than forty years old, others new, but I'm endlessly grateful to hear other people's stories. I still love to explore where we get stuck, what sets us free, and all of the rich, unique qualities in between that blend together to become our most potent gifts.

The point is that when we discover a shortcoming of ours, we don't have to waste a minute on self-hatred or negative self-talk. We must work from a supposition that we are worthy and deserving of love. All. The. Time.

On our ever-evolving life journey, we'll always notice there's a way of being that we'd like to change. Or, with self-awareness, choose an area in which we'd like to grow. When we approach this from a place of love instead of one of shame, then we develop the confidence to learn a new skill set in a relaxed and powerful way.

Yes, we may be learning something that seems unnatural for us.

And yet, when we take baby steps,
pause to breathe,
and enjoy the progress that we're making from a place of sufficiency,
we grow our confidence by flexing the muscles we didn't know we had.
We must send waves of love to ourselves for every small win.

I came across this quote in recent years from American poet, Christopher Poindexter, and I was like, *Where were you, buddy, when I was so filled with pain and uncertainty and believed that there was something wrong with me?* When I read it, I knew that I was not the only person who took up more than her assumed bandwidth; who was sometimes an over-sharer.

"You feel so much because you are so much."

Regardless of the package we come in, we need the lovers, the writers, the artists, the passion puppies, the storytellers, the long talkers, the mute scribblers, the songwriters who back up the stadium-fillers, the men who ugly cry. We need it all.

So, despite what anyone ever says to you — never stop feeling, connecting, dreaming, loving, and risking it all to be your True Self.

Kids know this when they are young. I knew it. I felt it, belting out my best Olivia Newton-John in the schoolyard. Then sadly, like so many of us, I allowed the volume to be lowered because somebody, somewhere was uncomfortable with my noise.

Eventually, though, the spirit needs to express itself. And so begins the hardscrabble journey back to the authentic self.

This can take years, involve many tears, and a whole lot of therapy. Or, we might change like flicking a light switch — but I'm here to tell you that there was nothing wrong with me in the first place, and there is nothing wrong with you.

And incidentally, "gentle" is the new "hustle".

> I can't hear the voice of love when I'm hustling. All I can hear are my own feet pounding the pavement, and the sound of other runners about to overtake me, beat me. But competition has no place in my life anymore. The stillness reminds me of that.[11]

This book is a love letter to you. And, as such, I've tried to put as many tender, sweet, loving messages in here as possible. Yet, if you remember one thing from this little book of outpouring love from me to you, please remember that there is no place for "hustling hard," or bragging about using the puke bucket at the CrossFit gym. These are just masks we wear to cover the fact that we're still afraid to accept ourselves as we are.

---

11 Shauna Niequist. *Present Over Perfect: Leaving Behind Frantic for a Simpler, More Soulful Way of Living,* (Grand Rapids: Zondervan, 2016, p.72).

Self-improvement is an obsession for many or at least an ongoing project. We're addicted to motion. We forget that no story is a straight line, and the mark of a good life is not a blood-tipped arrow.

Self-acceptance is not a war you're fighting in order to be seen, heard, or understood. It is an ease-filled practice where you look within and love what you find there.

Remember that exercise at the beginning of the book when I asked you to find your favourite childhood photo of yourself and study it? Why is that one your favourite? Why do you love that capture of yourself so much?

It's because you recognize in it the essence of who you truly were at that young age.

And love did not need to be earned.

You were worthy exactly as you were.

Well. You are still worthy.

I ask you: Are you striving now and constantly competing against others for the external validation that perhaps you could find on the inside?

I urge you to stop and ask yourself as you take another course, or cue up another podcast for your commute, or restrict the food on your plate, which version of yourself is driving you: Is it the lion tamer, or the open-armed Mama?

What I mean by this is — be honest. Are you knocking down goals because you're still afraid that you're not good enough, or do you do these things because you love yourself, and every minute of your life so damn much that you want to wrap yourself in richer and richer experiences?

There's a huge difference in motive here. Take a moment to examine your "why." Write in your journal any time your thoughts are muddled. Write until you understand why you're doing something. Pay attention to how you are speaking to yourself as you do it.

This whole approach is based on the science of the central nervous system and the biology of stress. Understanding how this works also removes some of the blame and shame that comes up for us as we've been rushing around trying to earn acknowledgement and grow our personal currency.

I'm going to stick to describing the basics of how our autonomic central nervous system works to make my point. Due to the chronic stress that so many of us live with at this time, so many of our beings are denied their full expression due to the amount of time that we dwell in the fight, flight, or freeze response. This is also called the *sympathetic* state, which I believe is poorly named because it's not actually that nice of a state to be in *all the time*.

This central nervous system state is activated often, or even continually, when we get stressed. Basically, when a threat is presented — and this could be a big dog lunging at us unexpectedly, or a constantly-irked boss breathing down our necks as we work through an unreasonable workload — hormones such as adrenalin and cortisol are released into our systems. These empower us to handle the stress by temporarily heightening our senses, sharpening our minds, and giving us a boost of physical strength.

The key work of the fight, flight, or freeze response of the sympathetic nervous system is meant to be temporary, though. And, during this chemical boost, other systems in our bodies need to take a little break so that the most

robust resources can head to the areas that will best serve us during a threat.

This means that our digestion and elimination take a time out.

So does our capacity for calm, slow processes. There is conflicting literature as to whether our immune system also takes a back seat at this time, but it's easy to see that our creativity and higher reasoning do as well. When we are in the sympathetic state of fight or flight, we are often fearful, stressed, and focused on what we don't have at that moment.

Once the central nervous system has perceived that the threat has moved on, we are meant to return to the *parasympathetic* state. The parasympathetic is also known as the Relaxation Response — during which time we feel safe and bountiful. We are now meant to have the energetic capacity to create art, cook a beautiful meal, have a long and meaningful conversation, and basically enhance the human experience.

This is perhaps an oversimplification of the process, yet hopefully you see the point I'm illustrating. It is challenging for us to enjoy beautiful, slow, and meaningful experiences and indeed apply the principles of this book when we are chronically stressed or scared out of our wits.

That's why I say, *Gentle is the new Hustle.*

If you want to get something done, be gentle.
If you want to learn something new, be gentle with your beautiful self.

Sufficiency versus scarcity.
Abundance versus lack.

Think *I am enough just as I am*, versus *I need to lose weight, I need to upgrade my skills, there's not enough money to go around, and there's only room for one of us at the top*. Don't live in a prison of your own making. Every day is a new one, with a chance to breathe and be. Approach everything you do with a soft-eyed, patient, and gentle focus on one moment at a time.

Remember that learning is vulnerable. It takes courage, mostly because we are all afraid of the criticism we will receive, or how weak we will look when we fail.

T. S. Eliot said, "If you aren't in over your head, how do you know how tall you are?"

Being uncomfortable won't kill us. Being criticized hurts, and definitely takes us off course sometimes. But if we courageously tap into the innately wise messages of our soul again and again, we'll find a life of joy and freedom. I'm hoping by now you know how to find those messages.

It's OK to act and make decisions with a tiny pit of nervousness in your belly, unsure of the outcome, and still go for it anyway.

Simply remember that you've got your Mama with you all the time. You are Mama to yourself. Give yourself a squeeze from within and remember that everyone has felt the same way that you do in your toughest moments.

Life is sexy, and fun, and challenging, but delightful, then painful, and then sexy and fun again. We might as well live it the way we want to.

So stand tall, spread your fingers and arms, reach out and up, and drink it all in. Each day is a gift to you, so live it.

Ask yourself: what does freedom feel like for you?

All I can say is, don't wait —
for it to be perfect,
for approval,
to be ready.
That day will never come.

I'd rather make big mistakes wading through my own bounty of imperfection than live shrivelled up by shame and fear.
How about you?

Beautiful Humans, will you simply be who you are alongside me?

Do you believe me now – there's nothing wrong with you?

LET

Don't be a good girl
And mindlessly follow the plan laid
out for you
and get married and make supper
and have kids and make lunches

So that one day you wake up and
remember that you forgot about
how you wanted to go North
in your VW van
and take pictures and write and listen
To the Earth —
for She shares her secrets only
when we are still.

And it's not about love or not
loving enough
and it's not about regret
It's about how eager you were to
quieten that voice
that might raise eyebrows, and make
heads shake side to side
that voice
that couldn't find it's roar
and how you were such
a people-pleaser
that you willingly strapped on that
straight jacket of compromise;

the one that keeps everyone happy,
and comfortable, and fed.

Instead, girl, let.
Let your hair loose
Let your hips move
Let the words fall out of your
mouth, uncensored
and let yourself be
where the laughter comes easily
as does your own truth.

Let it be art
Let it be power
Let it flow
And, dammit, let it be enough.

BIBLIOGRAPHY

Beck, Martha. *Finding Your Own North Star: Claiming the Life You Were Meant to Live.* New York: Three Rivers Press, 2001).

Brown, C. Brené. *The Gifts of Imperfection: Let Go of Who You Think You're Supposed to Be and Embrace Who You Are.* Center City, Minnesota: Hazeldon Publishing, 2010.

LaPorte, Danielle. *The Firestarter Sessions: A Soulful & Practical Guide to Creating Success on Your Own Terms.* New York: Harmony Books, 2012.

Maté, Gabor, M.D., *When the Body Says No: The Cost of Hidden Stress.* Toronto: Alfred A. Knopf Canada, 2003.

Niequist, Shauna. *Present Over Perfect: Leaving Behind Frantic for a Simpler, More Soulful Way of Living.* Grand Rapids: Zondervan, 2016.

Pressfield, Steven. *The War on Art: Break Through the Blocks and Win Your Inner Creative Battle.* New York: Black Irish Entertainment, 2002.

Sincero, Jen. *You Are a Badass at Making Money: Master the Mindset of Wealth*. New York: Penguin Books, 2017.

Twist, Lynne. *The Soul of Money: Transforming Your Relationship with Money and Life*. New York: W. W. Norton and Company, 2017.

*All names indicated as such have been changed to protect the anonymity of the person involved. You know who you are. Thank you for being my teachers.

CPSIA information can be obtained
at www.ICGtesting.com
Printed in the USA
BVHW082126280223
659395BV00002B/186